AWS Certified Alexa Skill Builder – Specialty Exam

200+ Practice Exam Questions with Answers, Explanations and References to prepare for the certification

Preparing for the certification

This Q& A book is supposed to supplement one's knowledge and fill in the gaps before appearing for the "Alexa Skill Builder – Specialty Exam", but by no means should be regarded as the principal material used for the preparation. We would hope the readers know well enough to not simply rely on this book, without having some hands-on development experience and rummage through the comprehensive documentation about the current Alexa platform (on developer.amazon.com). For more details and tips on the certification, feel free to visit http://alexacertprep.smarttechassist.com/

Disclaimer

We, the author and the publisher, have made every effort to ensure that the information in this book was correct and up to date at the time of publishing. However, we do not assume or claim any liability to anyone or any party for any loss, damage, or disruption caused by errors or omissions, whether arising out of negligence or any other cause. Please refer to the latest documentation on Amazon Web Services (developer.amazon.com) to make sure your preparation is up to date with the latest Alexa framework and features available, since the certification most certainly will pick-on latest features and framework available.

Gratias vobis agimus

We are grateful to many people, including many readers who provided and continue to provide feedback (esp. Corey Cotton for the voluminous feedback), during and after the publication of this book.

Contact us

We would love to continue to hear from all, to continue improving as well as attempt to keep the materials up to date, considering how fast things change. We hope this will provide all readers not only evaluate their understanding, but also to fill in any gaps in the certification process. If you find any issues, errors, or have any questions, feel free to reach us at smarttechassistorg@gmail.com.

Questions

Question 1 (Domain 1: Voice-First Design Practices and Capabilities)

Which of the following are not valid Alexa request types that a Skill Builder needs to handle while creating a skill? (SELECT THREE)

A. CanFulfillIntentRequest
B. OpenRequest
C. SessionEndedRequest
D. SessionStartedRequest
E. LaunchRequest

Question 2 (Domain 4: Skill Development)

A Skill Builder is configuring Login with Amazon (LWA) for a skill to allow users to log in with their Amazon credentials. Which of the user fields returned by the Alexa response should the Skill Builder use, in order to provide personalized content without risking exposing Personally Identifiable Information (PII) ?

A. profile:customer_id
B. profile:email
C. profile:name
D. profile:user_id

Question 3 (Domain 2: Skill Design)

"A Skill Builder has created a podcast skill "My Podcasts" using the AudioPlayer interface. What is the expected outcome after the last phrase from the user interaction as below?

User: "Alexa, play the latest episode from My Podcast Player"
User: "Alexa, pause".
User: "Alexa, resume"."

A. Alexa searches for the Latest episode and starts the audio stream
B. Depending on whether the skill timed out or not, Alexa will either play the current audio stream or fetch the latest episode from the podcast.
C. Alexa picks the most used audio skill and sends the AMAZON.ResumeIntent to that skill
D. Alexa sends the AMAZON.ResumeIntent and resumes the last played audio.

Question 4 (Domain 1: Voice-First Design Practices and Capabilities)

Which of the following objects should be part of all standard Alexa responses? (SELECT TWO)

A. version
B. sessionAttributes
C. response

D. display

Question 5 (Domain 4: Skill Development)

Under which tab in the Alexa Developer Console allows a Skill Builder to build the skill interaction model?
A. Build
B. Code
C. Test
D. Distribution

Question 6 (Domain 2: Skill Design)

If a card is included in the response to a touch event for a custom skill, will the card display in the Alexa app for the skill?
A. The card will display in the Alexa app
B. The card will not display in the Alexa app
C. Depends, if a Display.RenderTemplate directive is used, then the card will not show in the Alexa App
D. Depends, if a Display.RenderTemplate directive is used, then the card will show in the Alexa App

Question 7 (Domain 1: Voice-First Design Practices and Capabilities)

Which of the following methods are NOT available for StandardSkillBuilder object while using the ASK-SDK? (SELECT TWO)
A. addRequestHandler
B. withSkillId
C. withApiClient
D. withPersistenceAdapter

Question 8 (Domain 4: Skill Development)

Which of the methods are provided by the Alexa SDK to invoke the InSkill Purchase (ISP) API?
A. DirectiveServiceClient
B. MonetizationServiceClient
C. EndpointEnumerationServiceClient
D. ListManagementServiceClient

Question 9 (Domain 4: Skill Development)

A skill can send progressive responses from the context of which of the intent request types? (SELECT TWO)
A. LaunchRequest
B. IntentRequest
C. AudioPlayer.PlaybackStarted
D. CanFulfillIntentRequest

Question 10 (Domain 2: Skill Design)

Which of the ImageHelper class methods are provided by the ask sdk to help build text elements for use in Echo Show and other Alexa display compatible skills? (SELECT THREE)
A. withDescription()
B. addImageInstance()
C. getImage()
D. withPrimaryText()
E. getTextContent()

Question 11 (Domain 2: Skill Design)

Which of the following are valid custom slot types supported by Alexa?   (SELECT TWO)
A. AMAZON.DURATION
B. AMAZON.NUMBER
C. AMAZON.NINE_DIGIT_NUMBER
D. AMAZON.DAY

Question 12 (Domain 3: Skill Architecture)

Which of the following statements is NOT true regarding creating a skill as a web service endpoint?
A. The service must be accessible over the internet.
B. The service must support HTTP over SSL/TLS, using a trusted CA
C. The service must verify that incoming requests come from Alexa
D. You can use a custom web service only for custom and smart home skills.

Question 13 (Domain 2: Skill Design)

Which of the following is NOT true about the AMAZON.SearchQuery slot type?

A. Consider using the AMAZON.SearchQuery slot type to capture less-predictable input that makes up the search query.
B. Your skill can have as many AMAZON.SearchQuery slots per intent as needed.
C. Any sample utterance must include a "carrier" phrase (word or words that are part of the utterance, but not the slot)
D. An intent can have AMAZON.SearchQuery slot type in addition to other slot in sample utterances.

Question 14 (Domain 2: Skill Design)

How does the Entity Resolution help in mapping a user utterance to an intent resolution?

A. Enables a Skill Builder to add synonyms to your slot values and validate that a user actually said one of them. It resolves the synonyms to the slot values, so you don't have to write any code to match the synonym to the slot value
B. Creates new slot value for each of the synonyms added to the intent slot value, as the synonyms are used by a user.
C. Helps catch all of utterances as slot values, and provides a auto-handler to respond each time a synonym is spoken by a user, prompting the user to confirm if the he/she meant the word stored as the value of the synonym
D. Entity resolution takes place on built-in slot types "as-is", and the resolutions property is included on all values for the slot.

Question 15 (Domain 3: Skill Architecture)

Which of the following fields are part of the Account Linking Request JSON structure? (SELECT TWO)

A. accessTokenUrl
B. productid
C. type
D. productName

Question 16 (Domain 5: Test, Validate, and Troubleshoot)

A user is exiting a skill. Under which condition will the skill return SesssionEndedRequest as false?

A. An error occurs while the skill is in being used
B. The user utterance doesn't match the slot values defined for an intent
C. The user says "exit" or "quit".
D. The user does not respond while the device is listening for the user's response.

Question 17 (Domain 4: Skill Development)

ASK CLI command for getting a list of products associated with a specified skill ID
A. list-isp-for-skill
B. list-skills-for-isp
C. get-isp
D. list-isp-for-vendor

Question 18 (Domain 3: Skill Architecture)

Which of the following AWS services allows a Skill Builder to describe all the AWS services used by skill with infrastructure-as-code?
A. CloudFormation
B. CloudFront
C. Lambda
D. S3

Question 19 (Domain 3: Skill Architecture)

Which of the following AWS services allows a Skill Builder to setup continuous integration and continuous delivery (CI/CD) toolchain?
A. CloudFormation
B. CodePipeline
C. CodeStar
D. Lambda

Question 20 (Domain 6: Publishing, Operations, and Lifecycle Management)

The Skill description (visible on the Alexa app when browsing for skills) is defined in which field in the "Distribution" page in the Developer Console?
A. One Sentence Description
B. Detailed Description
C. Example Phrases
D. Keywords

Question 21 (Domain 6: Publishing, Operations, and Lifecycle Management)

How far back can I see the operational metrics for a skill multiple-choice
A. Since the skill publication date
B. Last 90 days
C. Last 6 months
D. Last 1 year

Question 22 (Domain 6: Publishing, Operations, and Lifecycle Management)

Which of the following metrics is NOT available "Smart Home" skill type?
A. Actions
B. Customers
C. Utterances
D. Sessions

Question 23 (Domain 6: Publishing, Operations, and Lifecycle Management)

Which of the following metrics are available for Earnings section in the Developer Console? (SELECT TWO)
A. Type
B. Payment Method
C. Earnings Before Tax
D. Total Payment

Question 24 (Domain 1: Voice-First Design Practices and Capabilities)

Which of the following statements is NOT true regarding Alexa-Hosted Skills?
A. Alexa-hosted skills support Node.js only
B. Alexa-hosted skills are limited to 75 Alexa-hosted skills in a single account
C. Alexa-hosted skills host all resources in US East for all locales
D. Alexa-hosted skills can be used for Custom skills and Smart Home skills.

Question 25 (Domain 4: Skill Development)

A skill has a subscription-based ISP, and the Skill Builder is considering a limited time free trial before asking users to make purchases to continue using the ISP. What option would be the easiest to accomplish this?
A. The Skill Builder can use set a trial subscription period from 0 to 31 days long
B. Create a separate free skill with limited ISP features, and encourage user to subscribe to the other skill to get premium features
C. Create a separate free skill , and encourage users to subscribe to the other skill to get premium features
D. Request Amazon to temporary remove skill pricing up to a specific date.

Question 26 (Domain 4: Skill Development)

A Skill Builder has created a skill for his business "TicketsOnline" with an invocation name "My Movie" which accepts small payments (upto $50 per transaction) to allow user to purchase movie tickets. The skill is also not child directed. What could a be potential reason for the skill to fail the certification process? (SELECT TWO)

  A. The invocation name must match the seller name (e.g. "Alexa, ask TicketsOnline for tickets to.."). If skill invocation name can't be changed, a new skill needs to be created
  B. The skill description is not updated to show which payment method (Amazon Pay or Account Linking) the skill uses for payment
  C. An Alexa skill can't accept Amazon Pay as a payment method
  D. It didn't ask customers to set a four-digit voice code to protect against unwanted or accidental purchases.

Question 27 (Domain 6: Publishing, Operations, and Lifecycle Management)

The owner of a developer account needs to provide access to another user so that the new user can view the Earnings & Payments reports but can't create or submit In-App Purchasing(IAPs). What kind of access can be provided to the user?

  A. Administrator
  B. Marketer
  C. Developer
  D. Analyst

Question 28 (Domain 5: Test, Validate, and Troubleshoot)

Which ASK SMAPI command can be used to validate a skill before submission for certification?

  A. "get-skill-validations""
  B. "submit-skill-validation"
  C. "submit-skill-for-certification"
  D. "validate-skill"

Question 29 (Domain 6: Publishing, Operations, and Lifecycle Management)

Which ASK API subcommand should be used to get the get list of all certifications available for a skill?

  A. get-certifications-list
  B. get-certification-review
  C. submit-skill-for-certification

D. get-skill-validations

Question 30 (Domain 3: Skill Architecture)
Which of the following statements regarding a lambda function is NOT true?
A. Lambda allows the Skill Builder to access and manage the servers it is running on.
B. AWS Lambda secures the skill code by storing in encrypted form in Amazon S3.
C. AWS Lambda may reuse an instance of function to serve a subsequent request, rather than creating a new copy.
D. AWS Lambda functions are stateless

Question 31 (Domain 1: Voice-First Design Practices and Capabilities)
Which is the following can be a valid skill invocation name?
A. sandra bullock
B. sandra's café
C. sandra 21
D. Sandra's skill

Question 32 (Domain 5: Test, Validate, and Troubleshoot)
Which of the following is NOT supported in the Alexa Simulator in the Developer Console?
A. Test the custom interaction model for a custom skill.
B. Device Display to see an approximation of how the skill displays on devices with screen.
C. Device Log to see the events sent to Alexa and the directives sent to the device during the skill interactions.
D. Enable Echo Buttons to display and interact with simulated Echo Buttons.

Question 33 (Domain 2: Skill Design)
Which of the following skill models do not support account linking?
A. Custom Skill
B. Video Skill
C. Baby activity model
D. Flash Briefing skill

Question 34 (Domain 3: Skill Architecture)

Which of the following statements regarding Amazon S3 is NOT true?
A. Total volume of data and number of objects one can store in S3 are unlimited.
B. One can store virtually any kind of data in any format in S3.
C. S3 offers multiple storage class options for different use cases.
D. S3 automatically enables versioning of any object stored to protect from accidental deletion.

Question 35 (Domain 2: Skill Design)

Which of the following Dialog directives should a Skill Builder use to ask Alexa to handle the next turn in the dialog with the user?
A. Dialog.ElicitSlot
B. Dialog.Delegate
C. Dialog.ConfirmIntent
D. Dialog.ConfirmSlot

Question 36 (Domain 2: Skill Design)

Which of the following display templates allow the use of hints? (SELECT TWO)
A. BodyTemplate1
B. BodyTemplate2
C. ListTemplate1
D. ListTemplate2

Question 37 (Domain 6: Publishing, Operations, and Lifecycle Management)

A Skill Builder is published a skill and would like to change the invocation name. What would be the best way to accomplish this?
A. Invocation name of a published skill cannot be changed. Create a new skill with the new invocation name and submit for certification.
B. The invocation name cannot be changed, need to create a new skill altogether with the new invocation name.
C. Edit the live skill and resubmit it for certification.
D. Using the ASK CLI use the "deploy" command to change the invocation name of a live skill.

Question 38 (Domain 2: Skill Design)

Which skill model allows a Skill Builder to create an Alexa-hosted skill?
A. Custom

B. Flash Briefing
C. Smart Home
D. Meetings

Question 39 (Domain 6: Publishing, Operations, and Lifecycle Management)
Which of the following is true regarding hiding a live skill from the Alexa store?
A. New users can enable the skill.
B. Existing users can continue to use the skill.
C. New users can search for the skill in the skill store.
D. Existing users can search for the skill in the skill store.

Question 40 (Domain 1: Voice-First Design Practices and Capabilities)
Which of the following is not a valid top-level object shared by directives (sent to a skill) and events (sent back to Alexa)?
A. Header
B. Endpoint
C. Payload
D. Scope

Question 41 (Domain 5: Test, Validate, and Troubleshoot)
A Skill Builder is making changes to the development version of a live skill and wants to publish to the changes to a select group of people to get feedback, before replacing the live version.
What is the BEST way to implement this requirement?
A. Publish the skill in a different locale and inform the select group to test the skill in the other locale.
B. Create a different skill with the change, publish the skill and inform the select group of testers to test the new skill.
C. Create a trial version of the skill for the selected group of users and have them test the skill, before publishing the skill .
D. Use the skill beta testing tool to send the skill to the group of users.

Question 42 (Domain 2: Skill Design)
Which skill models allow the Skill Builder to use the implicit grant for account linking?
A. Custom
B. Smart
C. Video
D. Music

Question 43 (Domain 4: Skill Development)
Which of the following statements is NOT correct regarding List Skills?
- A. A list skill can support account linking.
- B. Alexa customers share their lists with other customers within the same Amazon household
- C. "list_id" value remains unchanged if a list skill is disabled and then re-enabled.
- D. Customer can delete a default Alexa list.

Question 44 (Domain 6: Publishing, Operations, and Lifecycle Management)
Which of the following statements is NOT true regarding the utterance profiler?
- A. The utterance profiler can be used to test the dialog model.
- B. The utterance profiler does not call a web service endpoint for executing the skill code (lambda function or web service).
- C. The utterance profiler supports slot validation, slot confirmation, and slot elicitation.
- D. The utterance profiler can support both numbers ("9") as well as written-out numbers ("nine").

Question 45 (Domain 4: Skill Development)
For a music skill, which of the following are valid catalog types a skill can support? (SELECT TWO)
- A. AMAZON.BroadcastChannel
- B. AMAZON.Language
- C. AMAZON.MusicAlbum
- D. AMAZON.MusicEvent

Question 46 (Domain 1: Voice-First Design Practices and Capabilities)
A Skill Builder is designing a voice-based skill that provides a user with upto 30 seconds to answer a question.
Which of the following can help to fulfill this requirement?
- A. Add multiple re-prompts till the user responds.
- B. Set the "shouldEndSession" parameter to false.
- C. Use an audio clip with SSML tag audio
- D. Use the SSML "break" tag with the "time" attribute set to 30 seconds

Question 47 (Domain 3: Skill Architecture)

Which skill models mandate users to link their accounts before enable a skill? (SELECT TWO)
A. Custom
B. Smart home
C. Video
D. Flash Briefing

Question 48 (Domain 3: Skill Architecture)

Which of the statements are NOT true about an Alexa-hosted skill? (SELECT TWO)
A. Works only for custom skill.
B. You cannot add a library or a new dependency to an Alexa-hosted skill.
C. Session persistence is managed in an S3-backed key-value table.
D. An AWS account is required for an Alexa-hosted skill

Question 49 (Domain 2: Skill Design)

Which of the following are NOT required for a skill to provide multi-turn conversation? (SELECT TWO)
A. Intent confirmation
B. Dialog model
C. Session attributes to store user responses
D. Set shouldEndSession=false in the user response

Question 50 (Domain 5: Test, Validate, and Troubleshoot)

Which of the statements is not true about an example phrases for a custom skill defined in the skill store metadata?
A. At least one example phrase must be provided
B. Any example phrase(s) must come directly from the skill's sample utterances
C. Example phrases should not contain any emoticons, symbols, or grammatical errors
D. Example phrases must be all written in the primary language for the user locale

Question 51 (Domain 6: Publishing, Operations, and Lifecycle Management)

Which skill type does not provide the number of unique customers as a metric?
A. Custom
B. Smart Home
C. Flash Briefing

D. Music

Question 52 (Domain 1: Voice-First Design Practices and Capabilities)
A user is providing the following phrase to invoke a pizza ordering skill "Alexa, I want to order a large pepperoni pizza from Moe's Pizza ", which part of the phrase is the slot value?
A. Order
B. large pepperoni pizza
C. I want to
D. Moe's Pizza

Question 53 (Domain 6: Publishing, Operations, and Lifecycle Management)
How frequently is the operational metrics updated in the dashboard?
A. Weekly
B. Daily
C. Every 5 minutes
D. Every 2 hours

Question 54 (Domain 5: Test, Validate, and Troubleshoot)
Which of the following is NOT possible while testing a music skill?
A. Run a beta test.
B. Review the skill metadata (icon, description, etc.) in the Alexa App.
C. Test the skill on an Alexa device (linked to the developer account.)
D. Use the Skill Simulator API feature provided by the Skill Management API (SMAPI).

Question 55 (Domain 2: Skill Design)
Which of the following is a valid sample utterance for a custom intent?
A. Name the top 10 highest grossing movies of all time.
B. Has any aircraft broken travelled faster than Mach 2.2?
C. Where is the nearest atm?
D. How many calories in a small caramel frappé?

Question 56 (Domain 5: Test, Validate, and Troubleshoot)
A Skill Builder has created a skill in English (US). What could be a potential reason the English-speaking users in France not being able to find the skill in the skill store, even after changing their device language to "English(US)"? (SELECT TWO)

A. The skill has not been made available outside US.
B. The Skill Builder needs to publish a French version of the skill in the skill store
C. The skill code is deployed to a single endpoint, which supports the US region.
D. The skill doesn't have the skill code deployed to an additional endpoint to support France.

Question 57 (Domain 2: Skill Design)

A Skill Builder is extending the cancel section of their skill, but the sample utterances added are not triggering the built-in AMAZON.CancelIntent.

What is the EASIEST way to implement these phrases to trigger the section?
A. Replace the built-in intent with a custom intent.
B. Add sample utterances to the built-in AMAZON.CancelIntent.
C. Create a new intent replicating the skill exit behavior and map the sample utterances to the new intent.
D. Submit a ticket to Alexa Support requesting them to add the utterances to the AMAZON.CancelIntent

Question 58 (Domain 4: Skill Development)

A Skill Builder is creating a quiz-based skill using AWS Lambda, and wants to store the questions asked to the user during the game and number of questions the users got correct.

What is the SIMPLEST way to implement this requirement?
A. Persistent Attributes
B. Session Attributes
C. Storing state is not supported
D. Amazon S3

Question 59 (Domain 5: Test, Validate, and Troubleshoot)

Which of the following skill types cannot be tested in the test tab of the Alexa Developer Console?
A. Video Skills
B. Smart Home Skill
C. Custom Skills
D. Flash Briefing Skills

Question 60 (Domain 5: Test, Validate, and Troubleshoot)

Which of the following statements is correct regarding skill certification?

A. A skill Builder can "hide" or "remove" a skill after it is certified.
B. All skill types provide both the Validation and Functional Test sections for running pre-certification tests.
C. The functional tests are run automatically when a skill is submitted for certification.
D. A skill is considered "live" after it is certified.

Question 61 (Domain 4: Skill Development)

Which of the following the AudioPlayer interface requests, sent to an Audio skill with AudioPlayer interface, doesn't allow the skill to return a response to the request?
A. PlaybackStarted
B. PlaybackNearlyFinished
C. PlaybackFailed
D. PlaybackStopped

Question 62 (Domain 1: Voice-First Design Practices and Capabilities)

Which of the following statements is NOT true regarding Echo Button Skills?
A. An Echo Button skill can include support for either the Gadget Controller interface or the Game Engine interface, but not both
B. An Echo Button skill must be able to handle Echo Button press events along with voice responses and be able to share state information between the two invocation modes.
C. An Echo Button skill metadata will also display minimum and maximum number of players the skill supports, in the Alexa Skills Store.
D. An Echo Button skill can include support for the Gadget Controller interface, the Game Engine interface, or both

Question 63 (Domain 3: Skill Architecture)

Which of the following statements regarding DynamoDB is NOT true?
A. DynamoDB automatically scales throughput capacity as required.
B. DynamoDB provides asynchronous replication of data across multiple facilities, generally within a few minutes.
C. DynamoDB is a managed NoSQL database.
D. DynamoDB encrypts all customer data at rest by default

Question 64 (Domain 4: Skill Development)

Which of the following is NOT about voice purchasing using an Alexa skill?

A. An Alexa skill can allow purchasing of digital services or goods using In-Skill Purchases(ISP).
B. An Alexa skill can enable purchase of physical goods using Amazon Pay.
C. An Alexa user can turn off voice purchasing for the use account.
D. Amazon's return policies apply to purchases of non-digital products or services made through third-party Alexa skills

Question 65 (Domain 3: Skill Architecture)

A Skill Builder is creating a custom skill using lambda function as endpoint service. What configuration change should a Skill Builder introduce to ensure that a function can always reach a certain level of concurrency?

A. Reserved concurrency
B. Provisioned concurrency
C. Increase lambda function memory
D. Increase lambda function timeout

Question 66 (Domain 6: Publishing, Operations, and Lifecycle Management)

The skill icon on the Alexa app for a video skill is defined in which field in the "Distribution" page in the Developer Console?

A. Small Skill Icon
B. What's new?
C. Mobile App Icon
D. Large Skill Icon

Question 67 (Domain 1: Voice-First Design Practices and Capabilities)

A new skill being created needs to obtain the users email address. What is the EASIEST way to implement this requirement?

A. Leverage the Customer Contact Information API to obtain the email address
B. Use the customers email address inside the attributes section of the Session Object the skill receives when the intent is triggered.
C. Setup a server with OAuth authentication where the user can enter their email address. and then enable Account Linking for the skill. Use the Account Linking information to get the email
D. When the user first launches the skill ask them to spell out their email address. Store this in a Persisted Attribute

Question 68 (Domain 6: Publishing, Operations, and Lifecycle Management)

Once a skill is certified and published, which of the following cannot be done?
  A. Update your skill
  B. Hide your skill
  C. Remove your skill
  D. Change the invocation name

Question 69 (Domain 6: Publishing, Operations, and Lifecycle Management)

Which of the following metrics is NOT available for in-skill purchasing type "Subscription"?
  A. Purchases
  B. Offer Conversion Rate
  C. Churn
  D. Trial to Paid Conversion Rate

Question 70 (Domain 6: Publishing, Operations, and Lifecycle Management)

Which of the following might not be a reason for a child-directed skill to fail the certification process?
  A. Promotes any products, content, or services, or directs end users to engage with content outside of Alexa
  B. Sells any digital products or services without using Amazon In-Skill Purchasing
  C. Sells any physical products or services
  D. The skill encourages users to review or rate the skill

Question 71 (Domain 2: Skill Design)

A Skill Builder has an intent with multiple slots and does not want to handle any of the dialog in the code. What can be used to implement this?
  A. This feature is not available in the Alexa Console.
  B. Use the Progressive Response API.
  C. Enable auto delegation for the intent.
  D. Create an Alexa-hosted skill and enable auto-delegation.

Question 72 (Domain 6: Publishing, Operations, and Lifecycle Management)

A skill uses the AudioPlayer interface to stream audio. Which of the following might cause the skill to fail functional testing?
  A. Pressing a pause button (while audio is playing) on a supported hardware device stops the playback.

B. The skill plays audio that contains an Alexa wake word.

C. The volume of the audio playback does not vary significantly from normal Alexa text-to-speech.

D. For screen devices, the "play" or "pause" button resumes the audio playback.

Question 73 (Domain 6: Publishing, Operations, and Lifecycle Management)

Which of the following statements are not true about deploying a skill in multiple languages? (SELECT TWO)

A. Need to deploy the code to multiple endpoints

B. Can add additional languages to an existing skill.

C. It is not available for Smart Home skills.

D. It is not available for Flash Briefing skills

Question 74 (Domain 6: Publishing, Operations, and Lifecycle Management)

How frequently is the retention metrics updated in the dashboard?

A. Weekly

B. Daily

C. Every 5 minutes

D. Every 2 hours

Question 75 (Domain 4: Skill Development)

Which step is NOT required for implementing In-Skill Purchasing (ISP) into an existing skill?

A. Create one or more product(s).

B. Add ISP support to the existing skill code.

C. Add payment processing support to the existing skill code.

D. Submit the skill for certification.

Question 76 (Domain 6: Publishing, Operations, and Lifecycle Management)

A Skill Builder has creating a custom skill to stream audio using the AudioPlayer interface. He/she wants the skill to announce something like "Now Playing..." before the audio streaming starts. What would be the EASIEST way to accomplish this?

A. "Play" directive response will override any speech output provided, hence this is not possible.

B. Add the announcement to the OutputSpeech, Alexa speaks the provided text before beginning to stream the audio.

C. "Play" directive response doesn't support any standard properties such as outputSpeech, so this is not possible.

D. Record the announcement as an audio file. Create two Play directive requests, first one to play the announcement, and the second one to play the audio requested.

Question 77 (Domain 6: Publishing, Operations, and Lifecycle Management)

Which skill type allows a "Mobile App Icon" field to be added to a skill metadata, so that it can be displayed in the Alexa App on mobile devices?

A. Custom Skill
B. Smart Home Skill
C. Video Skill
D. Music Skill

Question 78 (Domain 2: Skill Design)

Which of the following are valid sample utterance for a custom intent? (SELECT TWO)

A. i'm exactly six feet tall.
B. The fastest time ever recorded in men's 100 meters sprint is 9.58 seconds.
C. What is the highest iq ever recorded?
D. Add some jalapeño toppings to my pizza.

Question 79 (Domain 3: Skill Architecture)

A Skill Builder is creating a custom skill using lambda function as endpoint service. What configuration change should a Skill Builder introduce to scale without fluctuations in latency as the usage goes up?

A. Use Reserved concurrency
B. Use Provisioned concurrency
C. Increase lambda function memory
D. Increase lambda function timeout

Question 80 (Domain 3: Skill Architecture)

What programming languages are supported by Alexa-hosted skills? (SELECT TWO)

A. Node.js
B. Java
C. Python
D. C#

Question 81 (Domain 4: Skill Development)

Which of the following is NOT a valid AudioPlayer request as supported by the AudioPlayer interface?
- A. PlaybackStarted
- B. PlaybackNearlyFinished
- C. PlaybackAlmostFinished
- D. PlaybackStopped

Question 82 (Domain 2: Skill Design)

Which of the following is the correct response code returned by the Alexa to a custom skill on successfully processing a Progressive Response directive request ?
- A. 204
- B. 429
- C. 400
- D. 401

Question 83 (Domain 2: Skill Design)

What will AMAZON.DATE data type convert user's utterance of "december twenty-third" into?
- A. "2015-12-23"
- B. "2015-23-12"
- C. "12-23-2015"
- D. "23-12-2015"

Question 84 (Domain 4: Skill Development)

Which of the following statements is NOT true regarding Entity Resolution?
- A. If you extend a slot type, entity resolution does take place and the resolutions property is included on all values for the slot.
- B. If you do not provide synonyms and custom IDs for a custom slot type, Entity Resolution doesn't take place.
- C. If the user's value matches one of your custom values or synonyms, the status code is ER_SUCCESS_MATCH
- D. If the user's value matches anything else (such as the built-in data for the type), the code is ER_SUCCESS_NO_MATCH

Question 85 (Domain 3: Skill Architecture)

Which of the following statements regarding a lambda function is NOT true?
A. One can use threads and processes in AWS Lambda function code.
B. Inbound network connections are blocked by AWS Lambda.
C. AWS Lambda supports using environment variables.
D. AWS Lambda allows a Skill Builder to scale the lambda function based on anticipated demand.

Question 86 (Domain 3: Skill Architecture)

Which of the Amazon S3 access control mechanisms allow an organization to create and manage multiple users under a single AWS account?
A. Identity and Access Management (IAM) policies
B. Bucket policies
C. Access Control Lists (ACLs)
D. Query String Authentication

Question 87 (Domain 4: Skill Development)

A Skill Builder is creating multi-modal skill using lambda function and uses an Amazon S3 bucket to host images for devices with display.

What is the LEAST required privilege for the images stored in Amazon S3 to be having to display on the screen-based devices?
A. Grant the AWS Lambda function READ access to the Amazon S3 Bucket
B. Make the image object publicly accessible in a private Amazon S3 Bucket
C. Make the image object private in a private Amazon S3 Bucket
D. Make both the Amazon S3 Bucket and the image object publicly accessible

Question 88 (Domain 1: Voice-First Design Practices and Capabilities)

A Skill Builder is designing a Flash Briefing using the Pre-Built Flash Briefing model. The Skill Builder wants the skill to start the flash briefing by greeting the user by his/her name.

How can the Skill Builder implement this requirement?
A. Add a custom intent to the skill and handle the intent in the code.
B. Flash briefing skills do not support this, create a new custom skill.
C. Use a webservice instead of lambda function to create the code to handle the intents.
D. Developer Console does not support this, use the ASK CLI to customize the intent for the Flash Briefing skill.

Question 89 (Domain 1: Voice-First Design Practices and Capabilities)

Which of the following top-level objects is NOT part of any Alexa request?
- A. version
- B. session
- C. context
- D. request

Question 90 (Domain 1: Voice-First Design Practices and Capabilities)

Which of the following is not a valid list event request type a Skill Builder can handle while creating a list skill?
- A. ItemsCreated
- B. ListUpdated
- C. ListCreated
- D. ItemsUpdated

Question 91 (Domain 4: Skill Development)

Which of the following methods are NOT available for CustomSkillBuilder object while using the ASK-SDK? (SELECT TWO)
- A. withPersistenceAdapter
- B. withTableName
- C. withApiClient
- D. withDynamoDbClient

Question 92 (Domain 4: Skill Development)

Which of the following fields are NOT part of Connections.SendRequest directive for an In-Skill Purchase (ISP) request ? (SELECT TWO)
- A. payload
- B. productid
- C. shouldEndSession
- D. skillID

Question 93 (Domain 5: Test, Validate, and Troubleshoot)

Which of the following statements is NOT true regarding the Alexa Simulator in test tab in the Alexa Developer Console?
- A. While using the Location Services, the answer will be null
- B. PlaybackController interface requests cannot be tested with the Alexa Simulator.

C. Device Display cannot be enabled to see how the skill displays on devices with screens.
D. The Alexa Simulator does not render the video playback while using the VideoApp directive

Question 94 (Domain 3: Skill Architecture)

Which feature of AWS lambda allows a single piece of code to be shared across multiple functions?
A. Layer
B. Alias
C. Version
D. Concurrency

Question 95 (Domain 6: Publishing, Operations, and Lifecycle Management)

Which of the following statements is NOT correct regarding Analyst role in the Alexa Developer Console?
A. An Analyst can view earnings reports
B. An Analyst can view sales reports
C. An Analyst can edit images and descriptions for skills
D. An Analyst can access the payments and earnings section

Question 96 (Domain 5: Test, Validate, and Troubleshoot)

The "Functional Test" section, on the Certification tab in the Alexa Developer Console, is not available for which skill type?
A. Custom Skills
B. Echo Button skill
C. Music Skill
D. Smart Home Skill

Question 97 (Domain 6: Publishing, Operations, and Lifecycle Management)

Which of the following metrics is NOT available for a Smart Home skill in the Alexa Developer console?
A. Actions
B. Retention
C. Customers
D. Utterances

©SmartTechAssist.com

Question 98 (Domain 5: Test, Validate, and Troubleshoot)

A Skill Builder has a live Alexa-hosted skill and needs to make a quick fix to the live code. However, the development version is undergoing further feature enhancements and fixes. Developer doesn't want this minor fix to merge with the development version and wants to put this temporary minor fix until the new version comes along. What would be the easiest approach?

A. Developer must make changes to the development version and submit the skill for re-certification

B. Developer must make changes to the development version and promote the code to live version (by clicking the "Promote to live" button in the code editor)

C. Since the code change is temporary and doesn't need to be saved for future, the developer can quick fix the live code directly to the live endpoint.

D. Clone the live skill to create a new skill and publish the new skill with the fix. Delete the skill later if needed.

Question 99 (Domain 4: Skill Development)

Which of the following is not a built-in intent for skills while using the AudioPlayer Directives?

A. AMAZON.PreviousIntent

B. AMAZON.RepeatIntent

C. AMAZON.PauseIntent

D. AMAZON.MusicPlaylist

Question 100 (Domain 4: Skill Development)

Which of the following items is NOT a requirement for accessing an audio file using the "audio" tag in SSML?

A. The file must be in MP3 format

B. The audio file must be less than 240 seconds duration

C. The file must either be publicly accessible or having the appropriate permissions to the lambda function.

D. MP3 must be hosted at an Internet-accessible HTTPS endpoint.

Question 101 (Domain 4: Skill Development)

Which of the following statement is NOT true regarding Slot Validation?

A. There can be multiple validation rules for a slot

B. Slot validation rules are only invoked when the dialog is delegated to Alexa

C. Slot validation rules allow comparison to a specific value (greater than or less than)

D. If a validation rule fails, Alexa completes checking all the remaining rules before prompting to the correct values for failed validation rules for any slot(s)

Question 102 (Domain 4: Skill Development)

Which of the following is NOT true regarding the behavior of skills for Alexa-enabled display devices using the Display Interface?

A. The default display template of BodyTemplate1 is automatically created and displayed if there is no template or card specified in the skill response, and none is currently displayed on screen.

B. One can have multiple Display.RenderTemplate directives in a response.

C. The textContent object allows for primaryText, secondaryText, and tertiaryText fields

D. If no template has been sent to the screen but a card has been sent, the card is displayed on the screen.

Question 103 (Domain 4: Skill Development)

An Alexa Skill Builder is debugging an AWS Lambda function using console.log() statements to inspect values passed in the requests. How can the log statements be reviewed by the Builder?

A. The log files can be viewed in Amazon CloudWatch.

B. The log files can be viewed in AWS CloudTrail logs.

C. The log files will be saved in S3 bucket.

D. The log files will be spoken by Alexa as part of outputSpeech response.

Question 104 (Domain 2: Skill Design)

Which of the following is not a requirement to create a Video Skill?

A. An AWS account

B. An Amazon developer account.

C. Understanding implementing account linking using OAuth 2.0

D. Understanding ISP implementation

Question 105 (Domain 4: Skill Development)

How can customers purchase in-skill products?

A. Via the Alexa App

B. On Amazon.com

C. Using the skill (containing the ISP)

D. Using either the skill or the Alexa App

Question 106 (Domain 3: Skill Architecture)

Which of the following are NOT required while hosting a Custom Skill as an AWS Lambda Function? (SELECT TWO)
A. Select one of the allowed AWS Lambda regions to host the lambda function.
B. Verify that the requests are coming from the Alexa service.
C. Implement the intent Request handlers.
D. Encryption of data transferred between lambda and Alexa service.

Question 107 (Domain 3: Skill Architecture)

Which of the following is NOT true regarding a Flash Briefing Skill?
A. Alexa might ignore older items.
B. For audio feeds containing multiple items, one can navigate to next and previous items by voice.
C. Feed text size can be unlimited, but Alexa will prioritize the feed output based on newer items in the feed.
D. Feed text doesn't support any special characters (e.g. HTML, XML, SSML tags)

Question 108 (Domain 1: Voice-First Design Practices and Capabilities)

A user is providing the following phrase to invoke a pizza ordering skill "Alexa, I want to order a large pepperoni pizza from Moe's Pizza ", which part is the Invocation Name?
A. Order
B. large pepperoni pizza
C. I want to
D. Moe's Pizza

Question 109 (Domain 4: Skill Development)

A Skill Builder us using SSML for outputSpeech and wants Alexa to pronounce the full name for any acronyms in the outputSpeech. Which SSSML tag should the Skill Builder use to for the acronyms?
A. say-as
B. sub
C. emphasis
D. phoneme

Question 110 (Domain 2: Skill Design)

Which of the following is the correct name for an intent?
A. Get2019BudgetIntent
B. Get.AnnualBudgetIntent
C. GetAnnualBudgetIntent
D. Get AnnualBudgetIntent

Question 111 (Domain 2: Skill Design)

Which of the following is not an acceptable for a custom slot type value?
A. Cornell Univ.
B. usb
C. AT&T
D. joe@example.com

Question 112 (Domain 3: Skill Architecture)

Which of the following is NOT true regarding the built-in List Skill type?
A. A list skill facilitates the use of list events in the skill service, so the skill can understand and react to changes to lists from top-level utterances on Alexa.
B. A list skill may include an optional custom component, which can include any features allowed for custom skills, in addition to list skill features.
C. Any changes to items in a list (adding, removing or updating an item) can trigger list events.
D. The Skill Builder can define endpoints to receive list events but can't define handlers for the list events.

Question 113 (Domain 2: Skill Design)

Which of the following is a valid sample utterance for a custom intent?
A. Share some $10 gift ideas.
B. Name the top 2 countries by annual GDP.
C. I plan to pursue an mba course next year.
D. I had cheese soufflé for breakfast today.

Question 114 (Domain 5: Test, Validate, and Troubleshoot)

Which of the following statements is NOT true regarding testing with the Alexa Developer Console?
A. One can select to test either the Development or Live stage of a skill.
B. One can test dialogs and entity resolution in the test tab of the Developer Console.

C. One can test how Alexa will speak any SSML text.

D. Can't test the skill for display devices which do not support video playback.

Question 115 (Domain 2: Skill Design)

Which of the following interfaces is required to be capture user events in a skill involving Echo Buttons?

A. Game Engine

B. Gadget Controller

C. Playback Controller

D. Display Interface

Question 116 (Domain 4: Skill Development)

A Skill Builder is creating a custom quiz game skill using AWS Lambda, and wants to skill to save where the user left the game and resume accordingly when the user wants to play the game again. Which type of attribute should be used to store the user progress information for the skill?

A. Persistence attribute

B. Session attribute

C. Request attribute

D. No attribute type will suffice, use a DynamoDB table to store the user information.

Question 117 (Domain 2: Skill Design)

Which skill type should a Skill Builder use to create a trivia-based game?

A. Smart Home Skill

B. Custom Skill

C. Video Skill

D. List Skill

Question 118 (Domain 2: Skill Design)

Which of the following statements is NOT true regarding the dialog model?

A. When a skill includes a dialog directive, it can use the built-in AMAZON.YesIntent or AMAZON.NoIntent

B. Alexa returns an IntentRequest during a conversation, while using the auto delegation.

C. Single slot-value sample utterances are allowed while using a dialog model for an intent.

D. When Alexa is confirming a slot, Yes and No responses can be handled with the Alexa dialog model.

Question 119 (Domain 2: Skill Design)
Which of the following is the correct name for an intent?
A. Get2019USHolidays
B. Get.USHolidays
C. Get US Holidays
D. GetUSHolidays

Question 120 (Domain 2: Skill Design)
Which of the following permissions are available for custom skills from the Developer Console (SELECT THREE)?
A. Device Address
B. Amazon Pay
C. Change Language
D. Reminders
E. Change Locale

Question 121 (Domain 2: Skill Design)
A Skill Builder is designing a Multi-Modal skill with images and a conditional workflow based on whether a user has a voice-only device or display device . What parameter in the "Context" object (in the JSON-format request from the user) should the Skill Builder use to know whether the device has a screen or not?
A. System.device.supportedInterfaces.Display
B. System.device.supportedInterfaces.VideoApp
C. System.device.supportedInterfaces
D. System.device.supportedInterfaces.Audio

Question 122 (Domain 4: Skill Development)
A Skill Builder is building a skill to accept donations for a charitable organization. What payment method must the skill builder implement to accept donation from users?
A. Subscription
B. Amazon Pay
C. Consumable
D. One-time purchase

Question 123 (Domain 2: Skill Design)
Which of the following statements is NOT true for a Custom Skill?
A. The Skill Builder can create an Alexa-hosted skill.
B. The Skill Builder defines the invocation name.

C. The skill can use custom intents and slots.
D. The skill transforms the utterances a user can say into requests that are sent to the skill.

Question 124 (Domain 5: Test, Validate, and Troubleshoot)

Which tab in the Developer Console allows a Skill Builder to create and update a skill's metadata (icon, description, etc.)?
A. Build
B. Distribution
C. Certification
D. Analytics

Question 125 (Domain 4: Skill Development)

Which of the following is NOT a valid Dialog Delegation Strategy option?
A. enable auto delegation
B. disable auto delegation
C. enable manual delegation
D. fallback to skill strategy

Question 126 (Domain 5: Test, Validate, and Troubleshoot)

Which of the following is NOT a limitation of testing a skill using the Alexa Simulator?
A. The Simulator does not allow testing for devices with screens that do not support video playback for skills.
B. The simulator cannot render audio playback, but only shows the AudioPlayer directives sent from your skill.
C. While testing a skill using the Device Address API on the simulator, the address fields show up as null.
D. The Alexa Simulator does not support testing flash briefing skills.

Question 127 (Domain 6: Publishing, Operations, and Lifecycle Management)

Which of the following would be acceptable for a skill to pass the certification process?
A. This skill is child-directed and allows the purchase of physical products.
B. Collects a user's health related information.
C. Skill provides health-related information but include a disclaimer in the description stating that the skill is not a substitute for professional medical advice.
D. Recommends other skills which are not owned by the same developer.

Question 128 (Domain 1: Voice-First Design Practices and Capabilities)

A Skill Builder is creating a custom skill with multiple intents and custom slot values. During testing, the Skill Builder realizes some of the sample utterances meant for one intent slot are triggering the wrong intents. How can the Builder debug what utterance was captured, what intent and the corresponding slot value it was mapped to?

A. Open the skill intent history to see what intent each utterance mapped to and the slot values.

B. Store the utterances and slot values to Amazon S3, then search the logs based on the testing time frame.

C. Log the utterances and slot values to Amazon DynamoDB, then query the logs after testing.

D. Log the event and slot values to Amazon CloudWatch, then review the logs after testing.

Question 129 (Domain 2: Skill Design)

Which of the following is NOT a mandatory component for building a custom skill?

A. Invocation Name

B. Intents

C. Sample utterances

D. Display interface

Question 130 (Domain 1: Voice-First Design Practices and Capabilities)

Which of the following are limitations to Alexa Response? (SELECT TWO)

A. The outputSpeech response cannot exceed 8000 characters.

B. The total size of the response cannot exceed 24 kilobytes.

C. Total size of the response doesn't have any limit by itself.

D. An image URL (smallImageUrl or largeImageUrl) doesn't have any size limit.

Question 131 (Domain 2: Skill Design)

Which of the following is NOT a valid parameter for the Card Object?

A. Type

B. Title

C. version

D. image

Question 132 (Domain 4: Skill Development)

Which of the following persistent adapters are available to store Persistent attributes with ASK SDK? (SELECT TWO)
A. S3PersistenceAdapter
B. SessionPersistenceAdapter
C. DynamoDbPersistenceAdapter
D. CloudFrontPersistenceAdapter

Question 133 (Domain 2: Skill Design)

Which of the methods is NOT provided by the ASK SDK for use with Text Content Helper classes to build text elements for use in Echo Show and other Alexa display compatible skills?
A. withPrimaryText()
B. withSecondaryText()
C. withTertiaryText()
D. textContent()
E. addImageInstance()

Question 134 (Domain 1: Voice-First Design Practices and Capabilities)

You are building a custom slot type to capture user input but are not sure if the various utterances the user might use, how would you handle the user intent requests?
A. AMAZON.SearchQuery slot type
B. FallBackIntent
C. Custom slot type for every possible utterance you can think of
D. Use entity resolution with all possible synonyms

Question 135 (Domain 4: Skill Development)

Which ASK SMAPI command can be used for adding a new in-skill product to a skill?
A. associate-isp-with-skill
B. create-isp-for-vendor
C. reset-entitlement-for-product
D. create-isp-for-skill

Question 136 (Domain 3: Skill Architecture)

Which of the following AWS services allows a Skill Builder to continuously deploy a skill from the source code repository?
A. CloudFormation

B. CodePipeline
C. Lambda
D. CodeStar

Question 137 (Domain 5: Test, Validate, and Troubleshoot)
Which of the following statements are NOT true regarding the Beta Test program?
(SELECT TWO)
A. You can't have a beta test version and a live version of the same skill at the same time
B. You can't customize the email messages sent to testers.
C. You cannot publish multiple version of the skill to different testers.
D. You can't update the beta version of the skill once the beta version is published

Question 138 (Domain 6: Publishing, Operations, and Lifecycle Management)
Which of the following statements is NOT true about skill metrics?
A. One can see the total metrics for a skill's all locales or languages in one place.
B. Number of unique customers and user enablements for a skill can be different
C. One can see skill metrics for skills in live or development stages.
D. Once can export the metrics data, but not the infographics (charts, grids, and other visualizations) for the skill

Question 139 (Domain 6: Publishing, Operations, and Lifecycle Management)
Which of the following metrics is NOT available in the Earnings section in Developer Console?
A. Refunds
B. Units Sold
C. Earnings Before Tax
D. Total Payment

Question 140 (Domain 2: Skill Design)
Which of the following statements is NOT correct regarding List Skills?
A. A customer cannot delete the default Alexa list
B. A customer can grant list read, but not list write permission.
C. If a customer of a list skill changes region, the skill won't work as a different regional API endpoint will be required for calling the List API.
D. There is no way for a Skill Builder to determine that an event has been triggered from their skill.

Question 141 (Domain 3: Skill Architecture)

What is the default behavior for users to enable a skill which uses account linking to connect to a third-party system?

A. Require users to link their accounts when they enable the skill.
B. Users can enable a skill without starting the account linking flow.
C. Account is linked during skill enablement; user can disable the account linking while enabling the skill.
D. User is given the option of "Link account later"

Question 142 (Domain 4: Skill Development)

A customer purchased a game product while using a skill. A few days later, he decides he is no longer interested in the product and requests a refund. What is the policy for refund for digital purchases? (SELECT TWO)

A. Digital purchases are not eligible for refunds.
B. Refund request for an ISP must be within 7 days of purchase.
C. Refund request can only be initiated in the Alexa app.
D. In the case of accidental purchases, customers may contact Amazon Customer Service to request a refund.

Question 143 (Domain 6: Publishing, Operations, and Lifecycle Management)

The owner of a developer account needs to provide access to another user so that the new user can create or submit In-App Purchasing (IAP) but can't manage user permissions. What kind of access can be provided to the user?

A. Administrator
B. Marketer
C. Developer
D. Analyst

Question 144 (Domain 2: Skill Design)

Which SMAPI subcommand should be used for updating account linking configuration information for a skill while the ASK SMAPI?

A. update-account-linking-info
B. upgrade-project
C. update-model
D. None of the above

Question 145 (Domain 2: Skill Design)

Which of the following are part of standard built-in slot types list is the English(US) locale? (SELECT TWO)
A. AMAZON.Color
B. AMAZON.Country
C. AMAZON.Rate
D. AMAZON.Currency

Question 146 (Domain 6: Publishing, Operations, and Lifecycle Management)

Which of the following might not be a reason for a health-related skill to fail the certification process?
A. Collects information relating to any Personally Identifiable Information(PII).
B. Contains the provision of health care to a person, or payment for the same.
C. Claims to provide life-saving assistance through the skill.
D. Provides health-related information or tips and includes a disclaimer in the skill description that the skill is not a substitute for professional medical advice.

Question 147 (Domain 1: Voice-First Design Practices and Capabilities)

Which of the following is a valid skill invocation name?
A. chicago
B. chicago sears
C. about chicago
D. chicago app

Question 148 (Domain 3: Skill Architecture)

Which of the following fields is not part of the Interaction Model root level JSON structure?
A. languageModel
B. intents
C. dialog
D. prompts

Question 149 (Domain 6: Publishing, Operations, and Lifecycle Management)

A skill uses the AudioPlayer interface to stream audio. Which of the following might be acceptable for the skill to pass the certification process during skill submission?
A. The skill includes materially different advertising than is included when the same content is made available outside of Alexa.

B. The skill includes audio advertisements using Alexa's voice.

C. Skill includes audio message informing customers of promotional offers in response to specific requests from users.

D. The skill includes audio advertisements using one of Amazon Polly voices.

Question 150 (Domain 6: Publishing, Operations, and Lifecycle Management)

A skill uses echo buttons to play a game. Which of the following will cause the skill to fail the certification process during skill submission?

A. When the skill first launches, it begins with a roll call that prompts users to wake their paired buttons.

B. If a player dropped off in the middle of gameplay, the rest of the players can continue playing the game.

C. User cannot use the skill without the echo buttons.

D. The skill provides LED animations on the buttons during gameplay.

Question 151 (Domain 5: Test, Validate, and Troubleshoot)

A popular skill is having an issue with one utterance that is triggering the AMAZON.FallbackIntent, even though it should trigger one of the defined custom intents. What would be the easiest way to resolve this?

A. Review and make changes to the "Unresolved Utterances" tab in the Intent History

B. Insert console.log() statements to log the details and review the CloudWatch logs for troubleshooting .

C. Test the skill by invoking the intents individually in the Developer Console > Test page

D. Create tests in the lambda console and test the intents in separate events.

Question 152 (Domain 4: Skill Development)

Which of the skill metrics for in-skill purchasing are not available for "Subscriptions" product type?

A. Churn

B. Offer Conversion Rate

C. Offer to Purchase Conversion

D. Trial to Paid Conversion Rate

Question 153 (Domain 2: Skill Design)

Which of the following is true regarding delegation strategy for your skill and intents while using a dialog model for an intent?

A. Dialog Delegation Strategy setting can be enabled at skill level.
B. Dialog Delegation Strategy setting can be enabled at intent level.
C. Dialog Delegation Strategy setting for an intent always overrides the skill-level Auto Delegation setting.
D. If skill-level Auto Delegation setting is enabled, it overrides and Dialog Delegation strategy.

Question 154 (Domain 4: Skill Development)

For skills built for display devices using the Display Interface, which tag in the text field of the TextContent object helps a to make the text selectable?
A. Select
B. Action
C. Display
D. Choose

Question 155 (Domain 2: Skill Design)

Which skill models allow a Skill Builder to define the requests a skill can handle? (SELECT TWO)
A. Custom
B. Flash Briefing
C. Smart Home
D. Video

Question 156 (Domain 1: Voice-First Design Practices and Capabilities)

What of the following statements is true regarding creating a private skill for an organization for use with an Alexa for Business account?
A. Private skills need to pass certification just as any other skill, before being published.
B. Private skill cannot be made available on shared devices, but users can be invited to join with their registered devices.
C. Private skills cannot be made available to users, they can only be made accessible on shared devices.
D. Private skills can be made available to other users and on shared devices.

Question 157 (Domain 3: Skill Architecture)

What AWS resources are included with an Alexa-Hosted skill? (SELECT TWO)
A. S3 bucket (for media storage)

B. Lambda endpoint
C. DynamoDB
D. Amazon EC2 instance

Question 158 (Domain 6: Publishing, Operations, and Lifecycle Management)

Which Alexa skill types provides "Account Linking Completion Rate" as a metric? (SELECT TWO)
  A. Custom
  B. Smart Home
  C. Video
  D. Music

Question 159 (Domain 4: Skill Development)

Which of the following AudioPlayer directives does results in Alexa sending a "PlayBackStopped" request to an audio skill created using AudioPlayer interface? (SELECT TWO)
  A. Stop (and Alexa identifies the request).
  B. When Alexa encounters an error when attempting to play a stream.
  C. User makes a voice request to Alexa while an audio is playing.
  D. The audio stream Alexa is playing comes to an end on its own.

Question 160 (Domain 4: Skill Development)

Which ISP product(s) requires one to choose a billing frequency?
  A. One-Time purchase
  B. Subscription
  C. Consumable
  D. Subscription or Consumable

Question 161 (Domain 4: Skill Development)

Which of the following is NOT true about AudioPlayer interface?
  A. A Skill Builder using the AudioPlayer interface and directives can extend the built-in intents with additional sample utterances.
  B. If a skill has started playing an audio, utterances such as 'stop' send the skill an AMAZON.PauseIntent instead of an AMAZON.StopIntent.
  C. A Skill Builder can only send one "Play" directive in a request.
  D. A response sent from a skill to a AudioPlayer request cannot include any of the standard properties such as outputSpeech, card.

Question 162 (Domain 3: Skill Architecture)

Which of the following statements regarding a lambda function version is NOT true?
A. A new version of Lambda function is created each time the function is published.
B. One can update the function code on the published version of a function.
C. The latest version of a function can be accessed using the function ARN and "$LATEST" suffix.
D. Lambda only publishes a new version of a previously published function if the code has changed compared to the last published version.

Question 163 (Domain 3: Skill Architecture)

Which of the following statements regarding CloudWatch is NOT true?
A. One can use CloudWatch Logs to store your log data indefinitely.
B. The minimum resolution possible for data received by CloudWatch receives is 1 second intervals.
C. CloudWatch does not support metric deletion.
D. CloudWatch metrics can be set up to be retained indefinitely.

Question 164 (Domain 2: Skill Design)

Which type of authorization protocol is supported with Account Linking for an Alexa skill?
A. OAuth 2.0
B. SAML 2.0
C. OpenID
D. OAuth 1.0a

Question 165 (Domain 2: Skill Design)

Which of the following features for a custom skill can NOT be changed in the Alexa App?
A. Change the "wake" word
B. Change the skill invocation name
C. Account linking to third party app.
D. Enable or disable a skill

Question 166 (Domain 2: Skill Design)

A Skill Builder wants to create a skill to ask an Alexa device with screen for a camera feed. Which skill type would be the EASIEST one to use?
A. Smart Home Skill
B. Custom Skill
C. Video Skill
D. Meeting Skill

Question 167 (Domain 2: Skill Design)

A Skill Builder is using the built-in slot type "AMAZON.Movie" to provide details about movies to its users. The skill builder wants to keep add new movies to the default list that comes with the slot type. What would be the easiest way to accomplish this?
A. Create a custom intent to store all movie names, without using the built-in slot type AMAZON.Movie as extending built-in slot types is not possible.
B. Create a custom slot type for the intent for storing all movie names, as built-in slot types do not allow adding values to the pre-defined list.
C. Create an additional intent (e.g. "List new movies") with slot values to capture the new movie names.
D. Extend the slot type to include new movies as custom slot type values.

Question 168 (Domain 2: Skill Design)

Which of the following is NOT a valid Response object method?
A. outputSpeech
B. card
C. prompt
D. shouldEndSession

Question 169 (Domain 2: Skill Design)

Which of the following is NOT a requirement for a skill using the Alexa Location Services?
A. The skill must not be a child-directed skill.
B. The skill includes a link to the Privacy Policy that applies to your skill on the Distribution page of the developer console.
C. The skill fetches previously stored location info for subsequent use, instead of fetching the latest location information every time a user invokes an intent that needs this information.
D. The skill must not use the location information obtained from this service to link the customer's account.

Question 170 (Domain 2: Skill Design)

Which of the following interfaces needs to be enabled in order to change the color of an Echo Button?
A. Game Engine
B. Gadget Controller
C. Playback Controller
D. Display Interface

Question 171 (Domain 2: Skill Design)

A Skill Builder is creating a skill to provide country specific information. Which of the following is a valid sample utterance while creating a custom intent?
A. How much is {Country}'s annual GDP?
B. Who is the {Position}-in-chief in {Country}?
C. Tell me about US-{Country} relations?
D. Who is in charge of the {Department} portfolio in {Country}?

Question 172 (Domain 2: Skill Design)

Which of the following statements is NOT true regarding the Dialog Model?
A. Slot confirmation is not mandatory for slots designated as "required".
B. Slot validation rules can be used with both required and non-required slots.
C. When an intent has multiple slots needing confirmation, Alexa controls the order in which the required slot values are asked.
D. Intent confirmation can be used to confirm the entire intent, along with all required slots for the intent.

Question 173 (Domain 1: Voice-First Design Practices and Capabilities)

A user is providing the following phrase to invoke a pizza ordering skill "Alexa, I want to order a large pepperoni pizza from Moe's Pizza ", what part is the intent in the interaction model?
A. Order
B. Large pepperoni pizza
C. I want to
D. Moe's Pizza

Question 174 (Domain 4: Skill Development)

Which of the following SSML tags is NOT supported Alexa Skills Kit?

A. Prosody
B. Sub
C. Lang
D. Mark

Question 175 (Domain 4: Skill Development)

Which of the following statements is NOT true regarding Entity Resolution?
A. The IntentRequest can include multiple possible matches for a slot.
B. When extending a built-in slot type, entity resolution does not take place.
C. Entity resolution can be tested using the "Test" page in the Alexa Developer Console.
D. When using a built-in slot type "as-is", entity resolution does not take place.

Question 176 (Domain 5: Test, Validate, and Troubleshoot)

A Skill Builder is creating a skill and is finding inconsistencies in triggering some of the intents. Some of the utterances for the built-in intent AMAZON.CancelIntent are triggering the "AMAZON.FallbackIntent".

What is the EASIEST way to resolve this issue?
A. Extend the AMAZON.CancelIntent to include the phrases that were not picked up by the AMAZON.CancelIntent.
B. Create a custom intent to send those specific phrases to the same handler as the AMAZON.CancelIntent.
C. Implement the CancelIntent with the additional utterances.
D. Built-in intents have pre-defined phrases and cannot be extended.

Question 177 (Domain 4: Skill Development)

Which of the following is NOT a type of in-skill products?
A. Consumables
B. Subscriptions
C. One-time purchases
D. Rewards

Question 178 (Domain 4: Skill Development)

For creating a music skill using the Alexa Music and Radio Skill API interfaces, which of the following is NOT a mandatory interface the Skill Builder needs to implement?
A. GetNextItem
B. GetPlayableContent

C. SetShuffle

D. Initiate

Question 179 (Domain 5: Test, Validate, and Troubleshoot)

Which of the following statements are true regarding the Skill Beta Testing Tool? (SELECT TWO)

A. A beta test can support unlimited number of testers.

B. The skill builder can receive feedback from the users.

C. The skill needs to be certified before using the tool.

D. A beta test can only last for 90 days maximum.

Question 180 (Domain 3: Skill Architecture)

Which of the following statements regarding a lambda function is NOT true?

A. Each alias has a unique ARN

B. It is possible to point an alias to two Lambda function versions based on certain conditions.

C. Once an alias is created, it cannot be updated to point to a new version of the function.

D. The alias cannot point to a function referred using $LATEST.

Question 181 (Domain 3: Skill Architecture)

A Skill Builder is creating a multi-modal skill with lots of images and expecting a large global audience. The skill needs minimal latency while displaying the images to the users. Which AWS Service would help to solve this requirement?

A. Amazon CloudFront

B. Amazon S3

C. Amazon DynamoDB

D. Amazon ElastiCache

Question 182 (Domain 4: Skill Development)

Which of the following is NOT a supported SSML tag?

A. Emphasis

B. Prosody

C. Voice

D. Pitch

Question 183 (Domain 6: Publishing, Operations, and Lifecycle Management)

A Skill Builder is unable to make any configuration changes to a live skill.
What is the most likely reason for this error?
  A. Any configuration changes to a live skill needs to be made the "development" version of the skill and sent for publishing as a new version.
  B. The Skill Builder might have enabled different regions on the Alexa Developer console while making the changes.
  C. The configuration changes might be violating Alexa policies for publishing a skill.
  D. The Skill Builder needs to send a request to the Amazon Support team to make any changes to a live skill.

Question 184 (Domain 3: Skill Architecture)

A Skill Builder wants a skill to log and alert on unexpected errors that may arise while users use the skill. Which AWS service would best fit this use case?
  A. Amazon S3
  B. Amazon CloudWatch
  C. AWS CloudTrail
  D. Amazon DynamoDB

Question 185 (Domain 4: Skill Development)

A Skill Builder is creating a skill and would like to use a different voice than the default Alexa's voice for responding to the user. What is the EASIEST way to implement this requirement?
  A. Send the OutputSpeech contents to AWS Polly to record as audio files and save them Amazon S3, and then include them in the response using SSML Audio tag
  B. Use the "Voice" tag in SSML.
  C. Use the "Speak" tag in SSML and use its " as" attribute.
  D. Record all possible phrases using a voice over artist, save and then host them as audio files on Amazon S3, and then include them in the response using SSML Audio tag

Question 186 (Domain 6: Publishing, Operations, and Lifecycle Management)

Which of the following statements is NOT correct with respect to the Marketer role in the Alexa Developer Console?
  A. A Marketer can edit images and descriptions for skills.
  B. A Marketer can access the Payments and Earnings section.
  C. A Marketer can access sales reports.
  D. A Marketer can create IAPs.

Question 187 (Domain 3: Skill Architecture)
Which of the following items are NOT required for Smart Home Skills?
A. Public name
B. Skill Description
C. Invocation Name
D. Example Phrases

Question 188 (Domain 4: Skill Development)
Which Alexa tool or framework can one use to create or manage a list skill?
A. Alexa Developer Console
B. ASK CLI
C. ASK SDK
D. AWS Console

Question 189 (Domain 6: Publishing, Operations, and Lifecycle Management)
Which of the following can cause a skill to fail the certification process?
A. A skill includes an audio message informing customer of promotional offers in response to specific requests from customers.
B. This skill is child-directed and allows purchase of digital products using Amazon In-Skill Purchasing (ISP).
C. A skill that requests users to leave a review or rating of the skill.
D. Allows customers to search for web content but doesn't attribute the source of the information.

Question 190 (Domain 6: Publishing, Operations, and Lifecycle Management)
Which of the following metrics is NOT available for custom skills in the Alexa Developer console?
A. Retention
B. Interaction Path
C. Utterances
D. Actions

Question 191 (Domain 2: Skill Design)
Which of the following skill types do NOT require an invocation name? (SELECT TWO)
A. Custom Skill
B. Music Skill

C. Flash Briefing Skill
D. Smart Home Skill

Question 192 (Domain 4: Skill Development)

Which of the following actions is NOT supported by In-Skill Purchase(ISP) addDirective?
A. Buy
B. Abandon
C. Cancel
D. Upsell

Question 193 (Domain 6: Publishing, Operations, and Lifecycle Management)

Which of the following skill information are available in the Amazon Alexa App? (SELECT TWO)
A. Alexa App Cards showing the skill description and other metadata
B. Alexa App History which shows every spoken interaction with Alexa
C. Skill Metrics which shows the skill usage stats
D. A skill's certification status

Question 194 (Domain 5: Test, Validate, and Troubleshoot)

A Skill Builder has published two versions of a skill to support English (US) and Italian (IT) languages. What could be a potential reason for the Italian users not being able to find the Italian version of the skill in the skill store, while the US version is accessible in the US?
A. The Italian version of the skill has not been made available in Italy.
B. The skill does not have the skill code deployed to an additional endpoint to support Italy.
C. The users located in Italy need to change the device language to English(US).
D. The skill code is deployed to a single endpoint.

Question 195 (Domain 3: Skill Architecture)

Which of the following intents CANNOT include the outputSpeech object in the response?
A. IntentRequest
B. LaunchRequest
C. Display.ElementSelected
D. SessionEndedRequest

Question 196 (Domain 4: Skill Development)

A Skill Builder is creating a music skill for display enabled devices as well. Which service interface needs to be enabled, so that users can send requests to the skill using touch controls on an Alexa-enabled device with screen?
 A. AudioPlayer
 B. VideoApp
 C. PlaybackController
 D. GadgetController

Question 197 (Domain 4: Skill Development)

Which SSML tag would a Skill Builder use in order to control how Alexa pronounces certain words?
 A. <say-as>
 B. <phoneme>
 C. <emphasis>
 D. <prosody>

Question 198 (Domain 3: Skill Architecture)

Which of the following statements is NOT true regarding testing a custom skill using the Utterance Profiler in the Developer Console?
 A. Requires skill interaction model to be created.
 B. Does not require service endpoint (lambda function or HTTPS web service) configured.
 C. Utterance profiler supports testing slot as well as intent confirmation.
 D. Utterance profiler supports testing slot validation.

Question 199 (Domain 6: Publishing, Operations, and Lifecycle Management)

An Alexa Skill Builder is creating a skill name with an invocation name of "online order checker" for an online ordering services onlineorder.org where users can check the status of their orders. The skill's main intent has the following sample utterances:
"what is the status of order {orderno}"
"what is the status of my order {orderno}"
"what is the arrival date of order {orderno}"
Which example phrase would be an acceptable for the skill?
 A. "Alexa, ask online order checker what is the status of the order 123456"
 B. "Alexa, ask online order checker what is the estimated arrival date of order 123456"

C. "Alexa, ask online order checker what is the status of my order 123456"

D. "Alexa, ask online order checker what is the status of my order number 123456"

Question 200 (Domain 5: Test, Validate, and Troubleshoot)

While testing for slot values in the Alexa Simulator tab in the Developer Console, which of the following is NOT a recommended input to get a valid date for the AMAON.DATE type slot?

A. "December 23 2019"

B. "December twenty-third"

C. "23 of December 2019"

D. "12/23/2019"

Question 201 (Domain 4: Skill Development)

Which of the following statements is NOT true regarding ISPs?

A. Customers can only make in-skill purchases using Alexa or amazon.com.

B. If a skill offers consumable products, the userId remains the same even if the user disables and re-enables the skill.

C. The ISP product can be of type Entitlements, Consumables or Subscriptions.

D. An ISP skill must be able to handle a user request to refund a purchase.

Question 202 (Domain 6: Publishing, Operations, and Lifecycle Management)

A Skill Builder made some changes to a previously published skill and is about to re-publish the skill. Which field (in the distribution page) must the Skill Builder update so that the updated version of the new skill shows up in the "Recently Updated" section of the Alexa app?

A. "Example Phrases"

B. "What's new?"

C. "Detailed Description"

D. "Keywords"

Question 203 (Domain 6: Publishing, Operations, and Lifecycle Management)

Which of the following statements is NOT true about skill metrics?

A. Metrics infographics like charts, grids can be exported as PNG or JPEG images.

B. Metrics are not available for meeting skills.

C. Metric data includes invocations from the Test page in the Alexa Developer console.

D. A Skill Builder can access skill metrics with the Metrics API.

Question 204 (Domain 4: Skill Development)

Which of the following statements is NOT true regarding skill events?

A. Skills events contain a "consentToken" field in the permissions object once a customer has granted the permissions to the skill.

B. Alexa will attempt to redeliver skill events if an acknowledgement is not sent by the skill service, for up to one hour.

C. There is no way a developer can confirm an event has been triggered due to their skill.

D. Skill events generated are delivered to a skill in the order they occurred.

Question 205 (Domain 6: Publishing, Operations, and Lifecycle Management)

Which skill type can be hosted on a custom Web Service?

A. Custom skill

B. Smart Home skill

C. Music skill

D. Any skill types

Question 206 (Domain 1: Voice-First Design Practices and Capabilities)

Which of the following items is optional for the interaction model for a custom skill?

A. Intents

B. Sample utterances

C. Dialog Model

D. Custom Slot Types

Question 207 (Domain 4: Skill Development)

Which of the following is NOT an option to manage a Skill interaction Model?

A. ASK CLI

B. SMAPI

C. Alexa Developer Console

D. AWS Console

Question 208 (Domain 3: Skill Architecture)

A Skill Builder is creating a skill and wants to store user interaction for subsequent uses. Further, the skill is expected to have a huge user base and the Skill Builder would like to have read–after–write consistency.

A. Use DynamoDbPersistenceAdapter
B. Use S3PersistenceAdapter
C. Use sessionAttributes
D. Use Request attributes

Answers

Answer 1: A, C, E

Valid Alexa request types:

(**Specific** – based on what you are trying to implement and enabling corresponding interfaces where applicable) AudioPlayer.*, CanFulfillIntentRequest, Connections.Response (purchaseResult), GadgetController.*, PlaybackController.*, InputHandlerEvent.* requests

(**Must**) IntentRequest, LaunchRequest, SessionEndedRequest.

For details, refer https://developer.amazon.com/docs/custom-skills/handle-requests-sent-by-alexa.html

Answer 2: D

"profile:user_id uniquely identifies the user but does not expose additional information beyond the User ID, which can be anonymous. The other fields returned are email, name and postal code.

Reference: https://developer.amazon.com/docs/login-with-amazon/obtain-customer-profile.html

Answer 3: D

If a skill is not in an active session but is playing audio, or was the skill most recently playing audio, utterances such as 'pause' send the skill an AMAZON.PauseIntent. AMAZON.ResumeIntent determine the previously playing track and send a new Play directive to restart playback

Reference: https://developer.amazon.com/docs/custom-skills/audioplayer-interface-reference.html#intents

Answer 4: A, C

Alexa response parameters include the version and response, while sessionAttributes is optional. "display" is not a valid response parameter.

For details, refer https://developer.amazon.com/docs/custom-skills/request-and-response-json-reference.html#response-parameters

Answer 5: A

Use Build to set up your skill, configure the interaction model, and specify the endpoints for your service.

Reference: https://developer.amazon.com/docs/devconsole/about-the-developer-console.html

Answer 6: B

Card, if included in the response to a touch event, never displays in the Alexa app.
For details, refer https://developer.amazon.com/docs/custom-skills/display-interface-reference.html

Answer 7: C, D

withPersistenceAdapter and withApiClient are only available on for customSkillBuilder object, not for the standardSkillBuilder object
For details, refer https://developer.amazon.com/en-US/docs/alexa/alexa-skills-kit-sdk-for-nodejs/construct-skill-instance.html#standardskillbuilder

Answer 8: B

ASK SDK for Node.js provides a MonetizationServiceClient that invokes the inSkillPurchase API to retrieve all in-skill products associated with the current skill
Reference: https://developer.amazon.com/docs/alexa-skills-kit-sdk-for-nodejs/call-alexa-service-apis.html

Answer 9: A, B

You end progressive responses from the context of a current LaunchRequest or IntentRequest only.
https://developer.amazon.com/docs/custom-skills/send-the-user-a-progressive-response.html

Answer 10: A, B, C

ASK SDK provides the following ImageHelper class methods to help you build image elements for Alexa supported display compatible skills: withDescription(), addImageInstance(), getImage().

https://developer.amazon.com/docs/alexa-skills-kit-sdk-for-nodejs/build-responses.html#image-and-text-helpers

Answer 11: A, B

"The following are valid custom slot types: AMAZON.DATE, AMAZON.DURATION, AMAZON.FOUR_DIGIT_NUMBER, AMAZON.NUMBER, AMAZON.TIME while the following are open to public beta (AMAZON.Ordinal, AMAZON.PhoneNumber)

For details, go to https://developer.amazon.com/docs/custom-skills/slot-type-reference.html

Answer 12: D

To handle requests sent by Alexa, your web service , the service must meet the following requirements: Be accessible over the internet, accept HTTP requests on port 443, support HTTP over SSL/TLS using an Amazon-trusted certificate, and verify that incoming requests come from Alexa. You can use a custom web service only for custom skills

Reference: https://developer.amazon.com/docs/custom-skills/host-a-custom-skill-as-a-web-service.html#requirements-for-web-service

Answer 13: B

Consider using the AMAZON.SearchQuery slot type to capture less-predictable input that makes up the search query. Your skill cannot use more than one AMAZON.SearchQuery slot per intent, and it can be used with other slots for the same intent. In addition, each sample utterance must include a carrier phrase. The exception is that you can omit the carrier phrase in slot samples.

Reference: https://developer.amazon.com/docs/custom-skills/slot-type-reference.html#searchquery

Answer 14: A

Entity Resolution Enables you to add synonyms to your slot values (custom or extend the built-in ones) and validate that a user said one of them. This simplifies your code since you don't have to write any code to match the synonym that user said to your slot value. The Alexa service will then handle resolving the synonyms to your slot values. When using a built-in slot type as is, no entity resolution takes place.

Reference: https://developer.amazon.com/blogs/alexa/post/5de2b24d-d932-4c6f-950d-d09d8ffdf4d4/entity-resolution-and-slot-validation

Answer 15: A, C

"The accountLinkingRequest structure is a JSON representation of the account linking information shown on the Build > Account Linking section of the developer console. The following are the fields in the JSON structure: accessTokenScheme, accessTokenUrl, AuthorizationURl, clientId, clientSecret, defaultTokenExpirationInSeconds, domains, reciprocalAccessTokenUrl, redirectUrls, scopes, skipOnEnablement, type.

Reference: https://developer.amazon.com/docs/smapi/account-linking-schemas.html

Answer 16: B

A SessionEndedRequest is an object that represents a request made to an Alexa skill to notify that a session was ended. The skill receives a SessionEndedRequest when a currently open session is closed for one of the following reasons: user says ""exit"" or ""quit"", user does not respond or says something that does not match an intent in the skill, or an error occurs.

References:
https://developer.amazon.com/docs/custom-skills/request-types-reference.html#sessionendedrequest
https://developer.amazon.com/docs/custom-skills/standard-built-in-intents.html#about-canceling-and-stopping

Answer 17: A

"list-isp-for-skill" command is for a list of products associated with a specified skill ID, "list-skills-for-isp" is to get the skills associated with a specified product, "get isp" is to get the in-skill product file or summary by product ID, while "list-isp-for-vendor" is to get a list of products associated with a specified vendor ID

Reference: https://developer.amazon.com/docs/smapi/isp-command-reference.html

Answer 18: A

CloudFormation allows you to use programming languages or a simple text file to model and provision, in an automated and secure manner.
Reference: https://developer.amazon.com/docs/aws-tools/create-and-manage-skills-with-aws-tools.html#aws-cloudformation

Answer 19: C

With AWS CodeStar, you can set up your entire continuous integration and continuous delivery (CI/CD) toolchain in minutes, allowing you to focus on your skill's code and start releasing code faster.

Reference: https://developer.amazon.com/docs/aws-tools/create-and-manage-skills-with-aws-tools.html

Answer 20: B

Detailed description is displayed in the Alexa app when users browse for skills.
Reference: https://developer.amazon.com/docs/devconsole/launch-your-skill.html#skill-metadata

Answer 21: B

You can view data for up to 90 days prior only.
Reference: https://developer.amazon.com/docs/devconsole/measure-skill-usage.html#faq

Answer 22: A

The following metrics are available for a Smart Home skill type: Actions, Customers, Utterances.
Reference: https://developer.amazon.com/docs/devconsole/measure-skill-usage.html#skill-metrics

Answer 23: A, C

The Earnings section displays the amount of earnings received from in-skill purchases or Alexa Developer Rewards each month. The Payments section displays payments made for in-skill purchases or Alexa Developer Rewards.
"Type" and "Earnings Before Tax" are metrics available   in the Earnings tab.

Reference: https://developer.amazon.com/docs/devconsole/view-payments-earnings.html

Answer 24: A, D

Your developer.amazon.com account can host upto 75 Alexa-hosted skills.

Alexa-hosted skills are available across all locales, though resources are hosted in the US East (N. Virginia) region.

Alexa-hosted skills currently supports Node.js(version 8.10) and (Python version 3.7).

Alexa-hosted skills can be used for creating custom skills only. You cannot use an Alexa-hosted skill to build a skill with a pre-built model.

https://developer.amazon.com/docs/hosted-skills/build-a-skill-end-to-end-using-an-alexa-hosted-skill.html#frequently-asked-questions

Answer 25: A

You can use set a trial subscription period from 0 to 31 days long. Setting the trial subscription to zero will result in no trial subscription being offered.

Reference: https://developer.amazon.com/docs/in-skill-purchase/isp-faqs.html#general-faqs

Answer 26: A, B

The skill must use Amazon Pay or account linking and must note in the skill description which one the skill uses.

If the skill uses account linking and sells an item(s) or transacts for $100 or more, it must give customers the option to set a four-digit voice code to protect against unwanted or accidental purchases.

https://developer.amazon.com/docs//custom-skills/requirements-for-skills-that-allow-purchases.html

Answer 27: D

Outside of an Administrator, Analyst is the only role that gives users the ability to view Earnings & Payments reports, but the role can't manage IAPs.

Reference: https://developer.amazon.com/docs/app-submission/manage-account-and-permissions.html#add_other_users

Answer 28: B

"*submit-skill-validation*" allows a skill developer to execute various validations against their skill, "*get-skill-validations*" provides the result of a previously executed validation, "*submit-skill-for-certification*" submits the skill for certification, while "*validate-skill*" is not a valid SMAPI command.
   Reference: https://developer.amazon.com/en-US/docs/alexa/smapi/ask-cli-command-reference.html#smapi-command

Answer 29: A

Use the ""get-certifications-list"" subcommand to get the list of all certifications available for a skill, including information about past certifications and any ongoing certification.
   Reference : https://developer.amazon.com/docs/smapi/ask-cli-command-reference.html#api-command

Answer 30: A

AWS Lambda operates the compute infrastructure on your behalf, allowing it to perform health checks, apply security patches, and do other routine maintenance. AWS Lambda stores code in Amazon S3 and encrypts it at rest. AWS Lambda may choose to retain an instance of your function and reuse it to serve a subsequent request, rather than creating a new copy for performance reasons. AWS functions are stateless by design to allow for rapid scaling as needed.

   Reference: https://aws.amazon.com/lambda/faqs/

Answer 31: B

Among the limitations on skill invocation names are: One-word invocation names not allowed, names of people or places (for example, ""molly"", ""Seattle"") are not allowed, characters like numbers must be spelled out (e.g. , ""twenty one""). unless they contain other words (for example, ""molly's horoscope""), must not contain any of the Alexa skill launch phrases(e.g. ""run,"" ""start,"" ""play,"" ""resume,"" ""use,"" ""launch,"" ""ask,) and connecting words, launch phrases (e.g. ""to,"" ""from,"" ""in,"" ""using,"" ""with,"" ""to,"" ""about,"" ""for,"" ""that,"" ""by,"" ""if,"" ""and,"" ""whether.""), must not contain the wake words ""Alexa,"" ""Amazon,"" ""Echo,"" or the words ""skill"" or ""app"". The invocation name cannot spell out phonemes. For example, a skill titled ""AWS Facts"" would need ""AWS"" represented as ""a. w. s. ""

Reference: https://developer.amazon.com/docs/custom-skills/choose-the-invocation-name-for-a-custom-skill.html#cert-invocation-name-req

Answer 32: A

Use the Utterance Profiler to test the custom interaction model for a custom skill. Alexa Simulator allows the following: Enable Device Display to see an approximation of how the skill displays on devices with screens, enable Device Log to see the events sent to Alexa and the directives sent to the device during the skill interactions, enable Echo Buttons to display and interact with simulated Echo Buttons (for skill using Echo Button)

Reference: https://developer.amazon.com/docs/devconsole/test-your-skill.html#use-simulator

Answer 33: D

Flash Briefing doesn't support account linking, while for custom skills, use account linking if the skill needs personalized data from another system

Reference: https://developer.amazon.com/docs/account-linking/understand-account-linking.html

Answer 34: D

Total volume of data and number of objects one can store in S3 are unlimited. One can store virtually any kind of data in any format. Amazon S3 offers a range of storage classes designed for different use cases (S3 Standard, S3 Intelligent-Tiering, S3 Standard-Infrequent Access and S3 One Zone-Infrequent Access, in addition to S3 Glacier for archival solutions). Users need to enable versioning for objects, and versions of an object also incur storage costs based on usage.

Reference: https://aws.amazon.com/s3/faqs/

Answer 35: B

Use Dialog.Delegate to send Alexa a command to handle the next turn in the dialog with the user.

Reference: https://developer.amazon.com/docs/custom-skills/dialog-interface-reference.html#directives

Answer 36: B, D

Only BodyTemplate2, BodyTemplate6, and ListTemplate2 templates support the Hint directive

Reference: https://developer.amazon.com/docs/custom-skills/display-interface-reference.html#full-json-response

Answer 37: A

You cannot modify the invocation name after the skill has been published and certified.

Reference: https://developer.amazon.com/docs/custom-skills/choose-the-invocation-name-for-a-custom-skill.html

Answer 38: A

Alexa-hosted skill is not available for any pre-built models

Reference: https://developer.amazon.com/docs/hosted-skills/build-a-skill-end-to-end-using-an-alexa-hosted-skill.html#setup

Answer 39: B

Users who already have the skill enabled will still be able to use it and continue to use as-is. Users who do not have the skill enabled will not be able to search or enable the skill once it is hidden.

Reference: https://developer.amazon.com/docs/devconsole/test-and-submit-your-skill.html#hide-or-remove

Answer 40: D

Both directives and events can contain the following top-level objects: Header, Endpoint, Payload

Reference: https://developer.amazon.com/docs/ask-overviews/understanding-the-different-types-of-skills.html

Answer 41: D

The skill beta testing tool is designed for the skill builder to test with a small group of people to get feedback before certification, and ideal for the scenario. There is no trial version of a skill.
Reference: https://developer.amazon.com/docs/custom-skills/skills-beta-testing-for-alexa-skills.html

Answer 42: A

The Alexa Skills Kit supports implicit grants for account linking only in custom skills, all skill models requiring account linking must use Authorization Code Grant.

https://developer.amazon.com/docs/account-linking/configure-implicit-grant.html

Answer 43: D

Customers cannot delete a default Alexa list but only delete the items from the default Alexa list. List skills support account linking. A list can be shared with other customers within the same Amazon household. ""list_id"" value remains unchanged if a list skill is disabled and then re-enabled.

https://developer.amazon.com/en-US/docs/alexa/custom-skills/list-faq.html

Answer 44: C

The utterance profiler can be used to test the dialog model; though it does not support testing slot validation but only slot elicitation, slot confirmation, and intent confirmation.
The utterance profiler does not call an endpoint, so you do not need to develop the service for your skill to test your model.
When you enter a test utterance, you can use either written form or spoken form. For example, you can use numerals ("5") or write out numbers ("five").

https://developer.amazon.com/docs/custom-skills/test-utterances-and-improve-your-interaction-model.html

Answer 45: A, C

The following are the types of catalogs supported by music skill type : AMAZON.BroadcastChannel, AMAZON.Genre, AMAZON.MusicAlbum, AMAZON.MusicGroup, AMAZON.MusicPlaylist, AMAZON.MusicRecording.

Reference: https://developer.amazon.com/docs/music-skills/catalog-reference.html#catalog-types

Answer 46: C

Audio tag lets you provide the URL for an MP3 file that Alexa can play while rendering or waiting for a response, upto 240 seconds. Re-prompt is allowed only once per response, and ""break"" tag can have a maximum time attribute of 10 seconds.

https://developer.amazon.com/docs/custom-skills/speech-synthesis-markup-language-ssml-reference.html#audio

Answer 47: B, C

As of now, Smart home, Video, Music (where account linking is supported), and Meetings activity skill types need account linking before a skill of these types can be enabled.
https://developer.amazon.com/docs/account-linking/understand-account-linking.html#is-account-linking-required

Answer 48: B, D

Alexa-hosted skill is available only for custom skill.
Session persistence is managed in an S3-backed key-value table. An AWS account is not required to provision the resources needed for an Alexa-hosted skill , unless the skill needs to use other AWS services or if the usage exceeds the AWS Free Tier limits. You can add a dependency or library to the package.json file within the AWS Lambda package for the skill.
Reference: https://developer.amazon.com/docs/hosted-skills/build-a-skill-end-to-end-using-an-alexa-hosted-skill.html

Answer 49: A, C

To create a multi-turn conversation, one needs to create the dialog model structure with slots, validation rules, prompts. as required. A Skill Builder can decide if intent confirmation is required for an intent needing multi-skill confirmation.

ShouldEndSession parameter in the Response object needs to be set to false keep the session open during a multi-turn conversation. Session attributes are not required when using a dialog model because the user's responses are sent to the skill in the intent's slot values.

Reference: https://developer.amazon.com/docs/custom-skills/dialog-interface-reference.html

Answer 50: D

At least one example phrase must be provided. Example phrases must come directly from the skill's sample utterances, and must not contain any emoticons, symbols, or grammatical errors. Example phrases are all written in the same language used by the Alexa account, not based on the user locale.

https://developer.amazon.com/docs/custom-skills/functional-testing-for-a-custom-skill.html#cert-example-phrases

Answer 51: D

The following skill types provide the number of unique customers as a skill metric: Custom, Flash Briefing, Smart Home.

https://developer.amazon.com/docs/devconsole/measure-skill-usage.html#skill-metrics

Answer 52: B

Users invoke a custom skill by using an Alexa-supported phrase based on the skill's interaction model in combination with the invocation name, and a request ("Alexa, ask Daily Horoscopes for the horoscope for Gemini").

Here it follows the pattern: <phrase><intent> <slot value>< <invocation name>

https://developer.amazon.com/docs/custom-skills/understanding-how-users-invoke-custom-skills.html

Answer 53: C

Operational metrics data is refreshed within every 5 minutes.

Reference: https://developer.amazon.com/docs/devconsole/measure-skill-usage.html#faq

Answer 54: D

Beta test is an optional step for a music skill before submitting for certification. Skill metadata can be reviewed in the detail page for the skill in the Amazon Alexa App (under the Skills option). Skill Simulation API can be used to simulate skill response to intents for custom skills only.

References: https://developer.amazon.com/en-US/docs/alexa/custom-skills/test-and-debug-a-custom-skill.html#general-testing-recommendations.
https://developer.amazon.com/en-US/docs/alexa/music-skills/testing-guide.html

Answer 55: D

The requirements of an utterance are as follows: numbers, symbols and punctuation marks should be spelled out ("five" not "5", "three point five stars" not "3.5 stars"), separate acronyms and other phrases by periods and spaces ("n. b. a.", not "nba"), include apostrophes in possessive and contractions ("romeo's" and "i'm"), include hyphens that are word-internal (""man-eating""), spell words with umlauts (ä, ü, ö) and sharp S (ß) correctly(e.g. "fußball" not "fussball").
For a detailed listing of requirements, refer the documentation below:
https://developer.amazon.com/en-US/docs/alexa/custom-skills/create-intents-utterances-and-slots.html#h3_intentref_rules

Answer 56: A, B

Users can choose a language they want to use for their devices if the skill supports it. However, to make a skill available to customers with an account registered in a different region, you need to add a new version (in the region's primary language) of the skill in the skill store, in addition to making sure the skill is available in the region. Example: to make a skill available to customers who use .fr accounts, you need to include a French version of the skill in the skill store.
You should deploy your code to multiple endpoints(based on location) for latency reasons, but this is not a must.
Reference: https://developer.amazon.com/en-US/docs/alexa/custom-skills/develop-skills-in-multiple-languages.html#h2-distribution

Answer 57: B

Extending the built-in intent is the easiest and recommended to increase a unified experience across Alexa Skills.

Create an additional (or custom) intent with sample utterances is a viable option but involve more work than simply extending a built-in intent with sample utterances.

Reference: https://developer.amazon.com/docs/custom-skills/implement-the-built-in-intents.html#extending

Answer 58: B

Session Attributes can store state within a session and is perfect for this scenario. Persistent Attributes and S3 would be an overkill since attributes are needed only for current session in the scenario described.

Reference: https://developer.amazon.com/docs/app-submission/manage-account-and-permissions.html#add_other_users

Answer 59: D

The Alexa Simulator does not support testing flash briefing skills.

Reference: https://developer.amazon.com/docs/devconsole/test-your-skill.html#alexa-simulator-limitations

Answer 60: C

A Skill Builder can "hide" or "remove" a skill after it is published, not just certified. The Skill Builder can determine when to publish a certified skill ("Publish Now" or "Publish On").

All skill types except Music skills provide both the Validation and Functional Test sections for running pre-certification tests. Music skills have just the Validation section.

A skill must pass Validation tests before running the functional tests.

The functional tests are automatically run when you submit your skill.

Reference: https://developer.amazon.com/en-US/docs/alexa/devconsole/test-and-submit-your-skill.html#validate-your-skill

Answer 61: D

PlaybackNearlyFinished and PlaybackFailed requests allow a skill to return any AudioPlayer directive responses, while PlaybackStarted can accept a Stop or

ClearQueue directive response. Your skill cannot return a response to PlaybackStopped.

None of the standard properties such as outputSpeech, card, or reprompt are acceptable for AudioPlayer responses.

Reference: https://developer.amazon.com/en-US/docs/alexa/custom-skills/audioplayer-interface-reference.html

Answer 62: D

Echo Button skills include support for the Gadget Controller interface, the Game Engine interface, or both.

Echo Button skill must be prepared to handle input that occurs outside of a voice interaction and keep track of any state information that needs to be shared between these two invocation modes. If a skill requires user to have Echo Buttons, it will be marked as ""Requires Echo Buttons"" in the Alexa Skills Store. The Alexa Skills Store will also list the minimum and maximum number of players that the skill supports, the minimum number of buttons that the skill requires, and the maximum number of buttons that the skill supports.

Reference: https://developer.amazon.com/docs/echo-button-skills/understand-echo-button-skills.html

Answer 63: B

DynamoDB is a managed NoSQL database, which automatically scales throughput capacity as required. DynamoDB provides synchronously replication of data across multiple facilities. DynamoDB encrypts all customer data at rest by default.

Reference: https://aws.amazon.com/dynamodb/features/

Answer 64: D

Alexa voice purchasing can be turned off from the Alexa app. Alexa allows a Skill Builder to use ISP for purchasing digital goods, and Amazon Pay for physical or non-digital goods. Amazon's return policies do not apply to purchases of physical products made through third-party Alexa skills (for instance, a food order placed through a restaurant's skill). Instead, the returns policy of the applicable skill developer applies, though it is covered under the Amazon Pay A-to-z Guarantee for qualified purchases of physical products made through third-party Alexa skills using Amazon Pay.

Reference:
https://www.amazon.com/gp/help/customer/display.html?nodeId=201602230

Answer 65: A

To ensure that a function can always reach a certain level of concurrency, you can configure the function with reserved concurrency.
Reference: https://docs.aws.amazon.com/lambda/latest/dg/configuration-concurrency.html

Answer 66: C

Mobile App Icon is displayed in the Alexa App on mobile devices for video skills.

https://developer.amazon.com/docs/devconsole/launch-your-skill.html#skill-metadata

Answer 67: A

Customer Contact Information API is the easiest way to implement this.
Session Object doesn't retain value beyond current session, asking customer to spell out is cumbersome and often inaccurately captured, while account linking is a viable solution, it is much more tedious and difficult to implement.

Reference: https://developer.amazon.com/docs/custom-skills/request-customer-contact-information-for-use-in-your-skill.html

Answer 68: D

Once a skill is published, you can update and re-submit the skill for publishing. You can hide a skill(only remains active for users who previously enabled it) or remove a skill(disabled for all users).

Reference: https://developer.amazon.com/docs/devconsole/test-and-submit-your-skill.html#publication-status

Answer 69: A

"Purchases" metrics is only available for "One-time purchases (entitlements)" and "consumables" type of ISP products
Reference: https://developer.amazon.com/docs/devconsole/measure-skill-usage.html#isp-metrics

Answer 70: D

A child-directed skill (skill is child directed if it caters to children and interacts with any user accounts the skill may maintain for children) mustn't promote any products or directs end users to engage with content outside of Alexa, sell any physical products or services, sell any digital products or services without using Amazon In-Skill Purchasing, collect any personal information from end users or includes content not suitable for all ages.

Any skill may encourage users to review or rate their skill, but may not explicitly request that users leave a positive rating of the skill

Reference: https://developer.amazon.com/docs/custom-skills/policy-testing-for-an-alexa-skill.html#cert-child-directed

Answer 71: C

Enable Auto Delegation to gather the input for the slots when enabled for the skill or intent.

Reference: https://developer.amazon.com/docs/custom-skills/delegate-dialog-to-alexa.html#ways-to-delegate-the-dialog-to-alexa

Answer 72: B

While listening to the audio playback, a supported hardware device should be able to stop the audio using the "pause" button.

If the skill plays audio that contains a wake word, skill needs to make sure the wake word in the audio doesn't wake up the device. Ensuring no pauses immediately after the wake word in the audio is one way to prevent this.

Reference: https://developer.amazon.com/docs/custom-skills/functional-testing-for-a-custom-skill.html#cert-audio-playback

Answer 73: A, D

Deploying the code to multiple endpoints is not required, but recommended for latency reasons, if applicable. If you choose to deploy your code to multiple endpoints, you must maintain the same code at all endpoints.

Deploying a skill in multiple languages is not available for Flash Briefing

Reference: https://developer.amazon.com/docs/custom-skills/develop-skills-in-multiple-languages.html

Answer 74: A

Retention metrics data is refreshed weekly.
Reference: https://developer.amazon.com/docs/devconsole/measure-skill-usage.html#faq

Answer 75: C

The following are the steps required to set up ISP in a skill: Create one or more in-skill products, add ISP support to your skill code, test your skill and submit it for certification. Amazon handles payment to the default bank account (provided in the Developer Console) once the payment and tax information is set up.

Reference: https://developer.amazon.com/docs/in-skill-purchase/isp-overview.html

Answer 76: B

You can send only one Play directive request.
When responding to a LaunchRequest or IntentRequest, your response can include both AudioPlayer directives and standard response properties such as outputSpeech, card, and reprompt. If you provide outputSpeech in the same response as a Play directive, Alexa speaks the provided text before beginning to stream the audio.

Reference: https://developer.amazon.com/en-US/docs/alexa/custom-skills/audioplayer-interface-reference.html#directives

Answer 77: C

"Mobile App Icon" is allowed only on Video Skill types.

https://developer.amazon.com/docs/devconsole/launch-your-skill.html#skill-metadata

Answer 78: A, D

The requirements of an utterance are as follows: numbers, symbols and punctuation marks should be spelled out ("five" not "5", ""three point five stars"" not ""3.5 stars""), separate acronyms and other phrases by periods and spaces ("n. b. a.", not "nba"), include apostrophes in possessive and contractions ("romeo's" and "i'm"), include hyphens that are word-internal ("man-eating"), spell words with umlauts (ä, ü, ö) and sharp S (ß) correctly(e.g. "fußball" not "fussball").

For a detailed listing of requirements, refer the documentation below:

Reference: https://developer.amazon.com/en-US/docs/alexa/custom-skills/create-intents-utterances-and-slots.html#h3_intentref_rules

Answer 79: B

To enable your function to scale without fluctuations in latency, a Skill Builder should use provisioned concurrency, so that all requests are served by initialized instances with very low latency.   Increasing lambda timeout or memory will not an impact on latency fluctuations.

Reference: https://docs.aws.amazon.com/lambda/latest/dg/configuration-concurrency.html

Answer 80: A, C

Alexa-hosted skills currently supports Node.js version 8.10 and Python version 3.7.

Reference: https://developer.amazon.com/docs/hosted-skills/build-a-skill-end-to-end-using-an-alexa-hosted-skill.html#programming

Answer 81: C

The list of AudioPlayer requests that are sent to a skill implementing the AudioPlayer are as follows:
AudioPlayer.PlaybackStarted, AudioPlayer.PlaybackFinished, AudioPlayer.PlaybackNearlyFinished, AudioPlayer.PlaybackFailed, AudioPlayer.PlaybackStopped

Reference: https://developer.amazon.com/en-US/docs/alexa/custom-skills/audioplayer-interface-reference.html#requests

Answer 82: A

Progressive Response API returns a 204 code once the progressive response is ready to be sent to the device

Reference: https://developer.amazon.com/docs/custom-skills/send-the-user-a-progressive-response.html#steps-to-send-a-progressive-response

Answer 83: A

AMAZON.DATE Converts words that represent dates into ISO-8601 date format. (YYYY-MM-DD)

Reference: https://developer.amazon.com/docs/custom-skills/slot-type-reference.html#date

Answer 84: B

If you extend a slot type, entity resolution does take place and the resolutions property is included on all values for the slot.

Entity resolution takes place on custom slot types even if you do not provide synonyms and custom IDs. In this case, Alexa assigns internal IDs to slot values.

If the user's value matches one of your custom values or synonyms, the status code is ER_SUCCESS_MATCH. If the user's value matches anything else (such as the built-in data for the type), the code is ER_SUCCESS_NO_MATCH.

Reference: https://developer.amazon.com/docs/custom-skills/define-synonyms-and-ids-for-slot-type-values-entity-resolution.html

Answer 85: D

AWS Lambda allows you to use normal language and operating system features, such as creating additional threads and processes. Resources allocated to the Lambda function, including memory, execution time, disk, and network use, must be shared among all the threads/processes it uses. Inbound network connections are blocked by AWS Lambda, and for outbound connections only TCP/IP and UDP/IP sockets are supported, and ptrace (debugging) system calls are blocked. One can use environment variables with AWS Lambda functions. AWS Lambda scales them automatically on your behalf.

Reference: https://aws.amazon.com/lambda/faqs/

Answer 86: A

IAM enables organizations with multiple employees to create and manage multiple users under a single AWS account.

Reference: https://aws.amazon.com/s3/faqs/

Answer 87: B

Images must be are publicly accessible , but the bucket hosting the images needn't be. The easiest way to do this declare objects "public" in a "private" bucket.

References:
https://developer.amazon.com/docs/custom-skills/display-interface-reference.html#image-size-and-format-allowed-by-display-templates
https://developer.amazon.com/docs/custom-skills/display-interface-reference.html#image-size-and-format-allowed-by-display-templates

Answer 88: B

Pre-Built models do not allow custom intents. For using a skill built using Flash Briefing model, a user can only ask for his/her flash briefing (by name), for the Flash Briefing skill enabled by the user. Further the only endpoint exposed and customized for a Flash Briefing skill is the feed endpoint.

https://developer.amazon.com/docs/ask-overviews/understanding-the-different-types-of-skills.html#skill-models

Answer 89: B

All requests include the version, context, and request objects at the top level, while the session object is included for all standard requests only, but not for requests associated with a specific interface (e.g. AudioPlayer, Display, etc.)

For details, refer https://developer.amazon.com/docs/custom-skills/request-and-response-json-reference.html

Answer 90: D

The following are the list events generated by a list skill type: ItemsCreated, ListUpdated, ListDeleted, ListCreated, ListUpdated, ItemsDeleted

https://developer.amazon.com/docs/smapi/list-events-in-alexa-skills.html

Answer 91: B, D

withTableName and withDynamoDbClient are only available on for customSkillBuilder object, not for the standardSkillBuilder object

For details, refer https://developer.amazon.com/en-US/docs/alexa/alexa-skills-kit-sdk-for-nodejs/construct-skill-instance.html#customskillbuilder

Answer 92: B, D

Connections.SendRequest directive consists of the following list of fields:
type, name, payload, token, shouldEndSession, upsellMessage

https://developer.amazon.com/docs/in-skill-purchase/add-isps-to-a-skill.html

Answer 93: C

Below are among the known limitations of the Alexa Simulator: Location Services can only display if user has enabled Location Services, Playback interface requests are not supported, does not render the video playback (only shows the VideoApp directives sent from your skill)

Reference: https://developer.amazon.com/docs/devconsole/test-your-skill.html#alexa-simulator-limitations

Answer 94: A

Code can be packaged as a Lambda Layer for sharing across multiple functions.
A function version is a copy of another version, while alias is like a pointer to a specific Lambda function version.

Reference: https://aws.amazon.com/lambda/faqs/

Answer 95: C

Refer to the four types of roles you can set for users (Administrator, Marketer, Analyst, Developer) and their permissions below:

Reference: https://developer.amazon.com/docs/app-submission/manage-account-and-permissions.html#add_other_users

Answer 96: C

All skill types except Music skills provide both the Validation and Functional Test sections for running pre-certification tests. Music skills have just the Validation section.

https://developer.amazon.com/docs/devconsole/test-and-submit-your-skill.html#functional-test

Answer 97: B

The following is the list of skill metrics are available for a Smart Home skill in the Developer console : Actions, Customers, Utterances

https://developer.amazon.com/en-US/docs/alexa/devconsole/measure-skill-usage.html#skill-metrics

Answer 98: C

If you want to make a quick fix to your live code and your development code has other changes that you do not want to promote for an Alexa hosted skill, you can make your fix directly to the live endpoint.

Reference: https://developer.amazon.com/docs/hosted-skills/build-a-skill-end-to-end-using-an-alexa-hosted-skill.html#endpoint

Answer 99: D

Refer to the list of built-in intents to be used for adding the AudioPlayer Interface below:

Reference: https://developer.amazon.com/docs/custom-skills/audioplayer-interface-reference.html#config

Answer 100: C

Requirements for a file accessible using the SSML audio tag are: The MP3 file must be hosted at an Internet-accessible HTTPS endpoint (with trusted SSL certificate), MP3 must be a valid MP3 file with no sensitive information, audio file not longer than 240 seconds, the bit rate must be 48 kbps, and the sample rate must be 22050Hz, 24000Hz, or 16000Hz

Reference: https://developer.amazon.com/docs/custom-skills/speech-synthesis-markup-language-ssml-reference.html#audio

Answer 101: D

You can create multiple validation rules for a slot.

You can configure a set of validation rules for a slot, along with prompts to use for slot values that fail validation. Alexa uses your slot validation rules when you delegate the dialog.

If a value fails a rule, Alexa stops checking and responds with the prompt to correct the value. In a set of multiple rules, a later rule is checked only when all preceding rules have passed.

Validation rules allows you to compare to values and synonyms defined for a custom slot type, to a fixed set of values, to a specific value (greater than or less than), or dates or times to a specified time span.

Reference: https://developer.amazon.com/docs/custom-skills/validate-slot-values.html

Answer 102: B

If no template has been sent to the screen, but a card has been sent, this card is displayed on the screen. The textContent object allows for primaryText, secondaryText, and tertiaryText fields for available templates.

The default template of BodyTemplate1 is automatically created and displayed if there is no template or card specified in the skill response, and none is currently displayed on screen.

Reference: https://developer.amazon.com/docs/custom-skills/display-interface-reference.html#textcontent-object-specifications

Answer 103: A

Lambda functions save log files to CloudWatch Logs by default. Logging entries are stored in CloudWatch. Logs by using standard logging statements such as console.log() in Node.js.

Reference: https://developer.amazon.com/blogs/alexa/post/37da1dc8-08a1-4a65-a964-762517f3ddd7/why-console-log-is-your-friend

Answer 104: D

In addition to an Amazon Developer account to create the skill, an AWS account is required to host the skill code as an AWS Lambda function. A connected device with cloud API. In addition, understanding how to link a connected device with a cloud API (or cloud-enabled video service) using OAuth 2.0 is required.

Reference: https://developer.amazon.com/en-US/docs/alexa/video/understand-the-video-skill-api.html#prerequisites-to-video-skill-development

Answer 105: C

Customers may only make in-skill purchases while using the skill at this time.

https://developer.amazon.com/docs/in-skill-purchase/isp-faqs.html

Answer 106: B, D

Using Lambda for hosting a skill removes some complexities as mentioned below: Do not need an SSL certificate, do not need to encrypt (Alexa encrypts its communications with Lambda by default), do not need to verify that requests are coming from the Alexa service(access to execute the lambda function is controlled by permissions within AWS instead). Instead, the lambda function can focus on handing intents and generating responses to the intent requests. Lambda function can be hosted only in one of the allowed AWS Lambda regions.

Reference: https://developer.amazon.com/docs/custom-skills/host-a-custom-skill-as-an-aws-lambda-function.html#about-lambda-functions-and-custom-skills

Answer 107: C

Alexa can ignore older items; hence it is important to verify that the date entries for the feed items accurately reflect the content date. In case of audio feeds, if it contains multiple items, one can ask for the next and previous items in the skill language. In case of audio feeds, feed exceeding the feed text size limit (currently 4,500 characters) is truncated to the nearest sentence under the feed text limit. Feed text must not content any special characters such as HTML, XML, SSML tags or nonstandard punctuation.

Reference: https://developer.amazon.com/en-US/docs/alexa/flashbriefing/flash-briefing-skill-certification-checklist.html

Answer 108: D

Users invoke a custom skill by using a phrase (supported by the Alexa service) in combination with the invocation name, and request for information (""Alexa, ask Daily Horoscopes for the horoscope for Gemini"").

Here it follows the pattern: <phrase><intent> <slot value>< <invocation name>
Preference: https://developer.amazon.com/docs/custom-skills/understanding-how-users-invoke-custom-skills.html

Answer 109: B

The "sub" specifies the pronunciation to substitute the word with the contents inside the alias attribute. The ""say-as' tag specifies how the text should be interpreted based on additional context provided and eliminate any ambiguity. Emphasis changes rate and volume of a speech, while phoneme provides a phonemic/phonetic pronunciation for the contained text.

Reference: https://developer.amazon.com/en-US/docs/alexa/custom-skills/speech-synthesis-markup-language-ssml-reference.html#sub

Answer 110: C

The name of the intent can only contain alphabetical characters and underscores. No numbers, spaces or special characters are allowed. Intent names cannot overlap with any slot names in the schema. Built-in intents use the AMAZON namespace, using a period, like this: AMAZON.HelpIntent. User defined intents should not use "AMAZON." or period(.) in the Intent name.

Reference: https://developer.amazon.com/en-US/docs/alexa/custom-skills/create-intents-utterances-and-slots.html#intent-name

Answer 111: B

Acronyms and initialisms, when used, are indicated using all caps or using lowercase letters separated by spaces and period. (e.g. USB or u.s.b.)

Reference: https://developer.amazon.com/docs/custom-skills/create-and-edit-custom-slot-types.html#custom-slot-type-values

Answer 112: D

A list skill is optimal for managing a skill for maintaining a list and can understand and react to changes that happen to lists from top-level utterances on Alexa.
Any changes to items in a list (adding, removing or updating an item) can trigger list events.

The Skill Builder can define endpoint to receive list events and handlers to process and respond to list events.

https://developer.amazon.com/en-US/docs/alexa/ask-overviews/understanding-the-different-types-of-skills.html#list-skills

Answer 113: D

The requirements of an utterance are as follows: numbers, symbols and punctuation marks should be spelled out ("five" not "5", "three point five stars" not "3.5 stars"), separate acronyms and other phrases by periods and spaces ("n. b. a.", not "nba"), include apostrophes in possessive and contractions ("romeo's" and "i'm"), include hyphens that are word-internal (""man-eating""), spell words with umlauts (ä, ü, ö) and sharp S (ß) correctly(e.g. "fußball" not "fussball").

For a detailed listing of requirements, refer the documentation below:

Reference: https://developer.amazon.com/en-US/docs/alexa/custom-skills/create-intents-utterances-and-slots.html#h3_intentref_rules

Answer 114: D

While enabling testing for a skill using the test page in the Developer Console, one can select either Development or Live stage from the drop-down list. Use the "Voice & Tone" tab in the test page to test how Alexa speaks plain or SSMLL text. Some devices with screens do not support video playback for skills. To test for display devices that do not support video playback skills, create a custom device and set Video Codecs to Disallow Video.

Reference: https://developer.amazon.com/docs/devconsole/test-your-skill.html#test-simulator

Answer 115: A

The Game Engine interface filters Echo Button presses into named events that it forwards to your skill, while the Gadget Controller interface enables skills to control Echo Buttons (e.g. change the color).

Preference: https://developer.amazon.com/docs/echo-button-skills/understand-echo-button-skills.html#incorporate

Answer 116: A

Request attributes last only till the request is served with a response, while persist throughout the lifespan of the current skill session only. Persistent attributes persist beyond the lifecycle of the current session and can be used for this purpose.

https://developer.amazon.com/docs/alexa-skills-kit-sdk-for-nodejs/manage-attributes.html

Answer 117: B

While a custom skill can handle any kind of request, none of the pre-built skill models mentioned in the options support creating a game.

https://developer.amazon.com/en-US/docs/alexa/ask-overviews/build-skills-with-the-alexa-skills-kit.html#what-kind-of-skill-do-you-want-to-create

Answer 118: B

A skill could include AMAZON.YesIntent and AMAZON.NoIntent to get yes/no responses within or outside of the dialog.

When you use a single slot within a dialog, Alexa can distinguish between the different steps of the dialog (slot elicitation, slot confirmation, or intent confirmation) to correctly route the "yes" or "no" reply.

Alexa supports and can route single slot value utterance depending on where user is within the dialog.

With manual delegation (**only**), the skill gets an IntentRequest for every turn of the conversation.

References:

https://developer.amazon.com/docs/custom-skills/dialog-interface-reference.html

https://developer.amazon.com/docs/custom-skills/use-a-dialog-model-to-manage-ambiguous-responses.html

Answer 119: D

The name of the intent can only contain alphabetical characters and underscores. No numbers, spaces or special characters are allowed. Intent names cannot overlap with any slot names in the schema.

https://developer.amazon.com/docs/custom-skills/create-intents-utterances-and-slots.html

Answer 120: A, B, D

The available permissions for custom skills in the developer console include: Device Address, Customer Name, Email, Phone Number, Lists Write/Read, Amazon Pay, Reminders, Location Services, Skills Personalization

Reference: https://developer.amazon.com/docs/custom-skills/configure-permissions-for-customer-information-in-your-skill.html

Answer 121: A

The event.context.System.device.supportedInterfaces.Display parameter indicates whether the user device supports display or not.

https://developer.amazon.com/en-US/docs/alexa/custom-skills/best-practices-for-designing-skills-for-alexa-enabled-devices-with-a-screen.html#parse-supported-interfaces

Answer 122: B

Use Amazon Pay for Alexa Skills to sell real-world goods and services such as food, clothing, donations, etc.

Reference: https://developer.amazon.com/en-US/docs/alexa/amazon-pay-alexa/alexa-amazon-pay-faq.html

Answer 123: D

Using a custom skill type a skill builder can define the requests(intents) the skill can handle, the interaction model(words users say to make (or invoke) those requests), the visual and touch interactions that users will experience and can invoke, as well as the skill invocation name. Some pre-built models transform the utterances to requests (e.g. Music Skills). Alexa-hosted skills are only available for custom skills.

Reference: https://developer.amazon.com/en-US/docs/alexa/amazon-pay-alexa/alexa-amazon-pay-faq.html#can-a-charitable-organization-build-a-skill-that-uses-amazon-pay

Answer 124: B

Use "Distribution" tab to manage the skill metadata and preview how your skill will appear in the skill store

https://developer.amazon.com/docs/devconsole/about-the-developer-console.html

Answer 125: C

Each intent that has a dialog model has an Dialog Delegation Strategy setting. This can be set to one of three options: enable auto delegation, disable auto delegation, and fallback to skill strategy.

Reference: https://developer.amazon.com/en-US/docs/alexa/custom-skills/delegate-dialog-to-alexa.html#configure-delegation

Answer 126: A

To test for devices with screens do not support video playback for skills, create a custom device in the Simulator and set Video Codecs to ""Disallow Video"". When using the Device Address API, address fields in the response are set to null and the postal code field is set to a default US postal code. The Alexa Simulator does not render the audio playback, but the Skill I/O section shows the AudioPlayer directives sent from your skill.

https://developer.amazon.com/en-US/docs/alexa/devconsole/test-your-skill.html#alexa-simulator-limitations

Answer 127: C

Child-directed skills can't sell any physical products or services. A skill can't recommend other skills not owned by the same developer. A skill can't provide or store a user's physical or mental health or condition. A skill providing health-related information must include a disclaimer in the skill description stating that the skill is not a substitute for professional medical advice.

Preference: https://developer.amazon.com/en-US/docs/alexa/custom-skills/policy-testing-for-an-alexa-skill.html

Answer 128: D

Intent History can be ruled out as an option as it needs users to provide input , further the data displayed is aggregated and anonymized, and must have at least 10 unique users per locale in a day for any data to be available.

CloudWatch enables monitoring and logging all events in AWS, is the easiest way to log and debug a skill as it allows one can see the entire request , including which intent was called by the user and the slot values that are being passed into the skill, and hence debug and test the utterance response.

Preference: https://developer.amazon.com/blogs/alexa/post/37da1dc8-08a1-4a65-a964-762517f3ddd7/why-console-log-is-your-friend

Answer 129: D

The following are the basic and mandatory components to be included in any custom skill: Intents that represent actions that users can do with your skill, set of sample utterances that specify the words and phrases users can say to invoke those intents, an invocation name that identifies the skill.

Reference: https://developer.amazon.com/en-US/docs/alexa/custom-skills/understanding-custom-skills.html#components-of-a-custom-skill

Answer 130: A, B

The following are the size limitations for the Alexa response:
The outputSpeech response cannot exceed 8000 characters.
Total text content included in a card cannot exceed 8000 characters. This includes the title, content, text, and image URLs.
An image URL (smallImageUrl or largeImageUrl) cannot exceed 2000 characters.
The token included in an audioItem.stream for the AudioPlayer.Play directive cannot exceed 1024 characters.
The url included in an audioItem.stream for the AudioPlayer.Play directive cannot exceed 8000 characters.
The total size of your response cannot exceed 24 kilobytes.

For details, refer https://developer.amazon.com/docs/custom-skills/request-and-response-json-reference.html#request-format

Answer 131: C

The following are the parameters for Card Object: type, title, content, text, image

Reference: https://developer.amazon.com/docs/custom-skills/request-and-response-json-reference.html#card-object

Answer 132: A, C

ask-sdk-s3-persistence-adapter package provides the following persistent adapters:

S3PersistenceAdapter, DynamoDbPersistenceAdapter

https://developer.amazon.com/docs/alexa-skills-kit-sdk-for-nodejs/manage-attributes.html

Answer 133: E

ASK SDK provides the following methods for use with TextContentHelper classes (RichTextContentHelper or PlainTextContentHelper) to help you build text elements for Alexa supported display compatible skills:

.withPrimaryText(), .withSecondaryText(), .withTertiaryText(), .getTextContent()
https://developer.amazon.com/docs/alexa-skills-kit-sdk-for-nodejs/build-responses.html#image-and-text-helpers

Answer 134: A

As you think about what users are likely to ask, consider using a built-in or custom slot type to capture user input that is more predictable, and the AMAZON.SearchQuery slot type to capture less-predictable input that makes up the search query. FallBackIntent is a catchall for everything else you can't handle, and while creating a Custom slot type is more predictable utterances that you can know of.

Reference: https://developer.amazon.com/docs/custom-skills/slot-type-reference.html#searchquery

Answer 135: A

"*associate-isp-with-skill*" SMAPI subcommand is to add a new in-skill product to a skill, "*create-isp-for-vendor*" is to create a new in-skill product for given vendor, "*reset-entitlement-for-product* " resets the entitlement(s) of the product for the current user, while "*create-isp-for-skill*" is not a valid SMAPI subcommand.

Reference: https://developer.amazon.com/docs/smapi/isp-command-reference.html.

Answer 136: B

With an AWS CodeCommit repository set up, you can use AWS CodePipeline to create a workflow that continuously deploys your Alexa skill from your source code repository.

https://developer.amazon.com/docs/aws-tools/create-and-manage-skills-with-aws-tools.html#aws-codepipeline

Answer 137: A, D

You can have a beta test version and a alive version of a skill at the same time. Live version is available to the general public, while beta test version is available only to selected testers.

You cannot customize these messages which are sent by Amazon from the console.

You cannot publish multiple version of the skill. You can update the beta version of the skill published

https://developer.amazon.com/docs/custom-skills/skills-beta-testing-for-alexa-skills.html#faq-for-the-skill-beta-testing-tool

Answer 138: D

One can see the total metrics for a skill's all locales or languages in one place. Number of unique customers and user enablements can be different, depending on how many unique customers have enabled and launched the skill.

Many metrics, including operational metrics, are available for skills in both the development stage and live stage.

One can export infographics (charts, grids, and other visualizations) as PNG or JPEG images.

Reference: https://developer.amazon.com/docs/devconsole/measure-skill-usage.html#faq

Answer 139: D

The Earnings section displays the amount of earnings received from in-skill purchases or Alexa Developer Rewards each month. The Payments section displays payments made for in-skill purchases or Alexa Developer Rewards.
"Total Payment" metrics is available in the Payments tab.

https://developer.amazon.com/docs/devconsole/view-payments-earnings.html

Answer 140: D

A customer cannot delete a default Alexa list, although a customer can delete all the items on an Alexa list.
A customer can grant list read or write permissions.
A customer can change regions without requiring a different API endpoint for calling the List APIs, as long as the customer doesn't change his/her preferred marketplace.
Skill Builder can determine that an event has been triggered due to their skill (by capturing the item_id returned by the Alexa event, generated by item create/delete request by the user.)

Reference: https://developer.amazon.com/docs/custom-skills/list-faq.html

Answer 141: A

A Skill Builder can require users to link their accounts when they enable the skill, but the default behavior is to enable a skill without starting the account linking flow.

https://developer.amazon.com/docs/account-linking/configure-optional-account-linking.html

Answer 142: A, D

Digital purchases (including mobile apps, video, and music) are not eligible for refunds. In the case of accidental purchases, customers may contact Amazon Customer Service to request a refund.

Reference: https://developer.amazon.com/docs/in-skill-purchase/isp-faqs.html

Answer 143: B

Outside of an Administrator, Marketer is the only role that gives users the ability to manage IAPs, but the role can't manage user permissions.

Reference: https://developer.amazon.com/docs/app-submission/manage-account-and-permissions.html#add_other_users

Answer 144: A

Use the "*ask smapi update-account-linking-info*" subcommand to updating account linking information.

Reference: https://developer.amazon.com/en-US/docs/alexa/smapi/ask-cli-command-reference.html#update-account-linking-info-subcommand

Answer 145: A, B

Refer to the list of all built-in slot types across locales below. Some are in public (beta testing) phase.

Reference: https://developer.amazon.com/docs/custom-skills/slot-type-reference.html#list-slot-types

Answer 146: D

A skill should not collect any PII, the provision of health care to a person, or payment for the same, must not claims to provide life-saving assistance through the skill, and provides health-related information with a disclaimer in the skill description stating that the skill is not a substitute for professional medical advice.

Reference: https://developer.amazon.com/docs/custom-skills/policy-testing-for-an-alexa-skill.html#3-health

Answer 147: B

Among the limitations on skill invocation names are: One-word invocation names not allowed, names of people or places (for example, "molly", "Seattle") are not allowed, unless they contain other words (for example, "molly's horoscope"), must not contain any of the Alexa skill launch phrases(e.g. "run", "start" ,"play", "resume", "use", "launch", "ask") and connecting words, launch phrases (e.g. "to", "from", "in", "using", "with", "to", "about", "for", "that", "by", "if", "and", "whether"), must not contain the wake words "Alexa", "Amazon", "Echo" or the words "skill" or "app".

Reference: https://developer.amazon.com/docs/custom-skills/choose-the-invocation-name-for-a-custom-skill.html#cert-invocation-name-req

Answer 148: B

The following are the fields in the Interaction Model JSON structure: languageModel, dialog, prompts

Reference: https://developer.amazon.com/docs/smapi/interaction-model-schema.html

Answer 149: C

Streaming music/radio/podcast or flash briefing skills may include audio advertisements as long as the advertisements do not use Alexa's voice, Amazon Polly voices, or a similar voice, refer to Alexa, or imitate Alexa interactions and the skill does not include more or materially different advertising than is included when the same or similar content is made available outside of Alexa.

Skills may include audio messaging informing customers of promotional offers or deals in response to specific requests from customers.

Reference: https://developer.amazon.com/docs/custom-skills/policy-testing-for-an-alexa-skill.html#5-advertising

Answer 150: C

When the skill first launches, it must begin with a roll call that prompts users to wake their paired buttons (can skip roll call if launched within ten minutes of a previous session of the skill). If a player is dropped in the middle of gameplay, the rest of the players should be able to continue playing the game.

The user must be able to use the skill without buttons.

The skill must also ask the user before roll call or during roll call whether the user wants to play with or without buttons.

The skill must use LED colors on the buttons to provide an interactive experience to the users.

Reference: https://developer.amazon.com/docs/custom-skills/functional-testing-for-a-custom-skill.html#cert-echo-buttons

Answer 151: A

Since it is known that one utterance is not correctly triggering the right intent, its easiest to review the Intent History for the utterances and make the mapping changes for utterances to intents there itself. Review the "Unresolved Utterances" tab and either map it to an intent or slot as appropriate.

Reference: https://developer.amazon.com/docs/custom-skills/review-intent-history-devconsole.html#review-and-resolve

Answer 152: C

"Churn" represents the percentage of active paid subscriptions that expired or canceled. "Offer Conversion Rate" is the percentage of offer impressions that resulted in the customer signing up for a new trial or paid subscription. "Trial to Paid Conversion" Rate represents the percentage of trials that became paid subscriptions.

"Offer to Purchase Conversion " represents percentage of offer impressions that resulted in a purchase and is applicable to one-time purchases (entitlements) and consumables.

Reference: https://developer.amazon.com/docs/devconsole/measure-skill-usage.html#subscriptions

Answer 153: C

Every skill has a skill-level Auto Delegation setting, which can be either enabled or disabled. Auto-Delegation is enabled by default for a new skill. Each intent that has a dialog model has a Dialog Delegation Strategy setting, which always takes precedence over the skill-level Auto Delegation setting.

https://developer.amazon.com/docs/custom-skills/delegate-dialog-to-alexa.html#configure-delegation

Answer 154: B

In the "text" field, you can include text that is wrapped in an "action" tag, which is then selectable on the screen. "Select", "display", "choose" are not valid tags for use in the text field of textContent Object.

Reference: https://developer.amazon.com/docs/custom-skills/display-interface-reference.html#textcontent-object-specifications

Answer 155: A, D

For custom skill as well as Video skill, the Skill Builder can define requests the skill can handle (for video skill , requests such as such as playing and searching for video content and how video content search results display.)

Reference: https://developer.amazon.com/docs/ask-overviews/understanding-the-different-types-of-skills.html

Answer 156: D

Private skills are not subject to certification. As a result, you should only enable private skills that you developed or are from trusted developers. A private skill can be made available to shared devices by adding the skill to a skill group and then adding the skill group to your rooms. To make a private skill available to users after publishing, check the "Available for users" in the Alexa for Business Console.

Reference: https://aws.amazon.com/alexaforbusiness/faqs/

Answer 157: A, B

The following resources are included in an Alexa-hosted skill: Lambda endpoint, an S3 bucket for media storage, and Amazon S3-backed key-value table for managing session persistence.In addition, the service also sets up an AWS CodeCommit repository for managing your code.

Reference: https://developer.amazon.com/docs/hosted-skills/build-a-skill-end-to-end-using-an-alexa-hosted-skill.html#setup

Answer 158: A, B

Smart home and custom skill provide the ""Account Linking Completion Rate"" metric.

Reference: https://developer.amazon.com/docs/devconsole/measure-skill-usage.html#skill-metrics

Answer 159: A, C

Alexa sends PlaybackStopped request in response to one of the following AudioPlayer directives: Stop, Play (with a playBehavior of REPLACE_ALL), or

ClearQueue (with a clearBehavior of CLEAR_ALL). This request is also sent if the user makes a voice request to Alexa, since this temporarily pauses the playback.

Alexa sends a PlaybackFailed request Sent when Alexa encounters an error when attempting to play a stream.

Reference: https://developer.amazon.com/en-US/docs/alexa/custom-skills/audioplayer-interface-reference.html#playbackstopped

Answer 160: B

Billing frequency is applicable to Subscriptions only, and indicates how often the customer is billed for the subscription (Monthly/Yearly)

Reference: https://developer.amazon.com/docs/in-skill-purchase/create-isp-dev-console.html#billing-fields

Answer 161: A

You cannot extend the above built-in intents with your own sample utterances. When your skill is not in an active session but is playing audio, or was the skill most recently playing audio, utterances such as 'stop' send your skill an AMAZON.PauseIntent instead of an AMAZON.StopIntent. You can only send one Play directive in a request. When responding to AudioPlayer requests, you can only respond with AudioPlayer directives. The response cannot include any of the standard properties such as outputSpeech

Reference: https://developer.amazon.com/en-US/docs/alexa/custom-skills/audioplayer-interface-reference.html#requests

Answer 162: B

The system creates a new version of your Lambda function each time that you publish the function. You can change the function code and settings only on the unpublished version of a function. When you publish a version, the code and most of the settings are locked to ensure a consistent experience for users of that version. The latest version of a function can be accessed using the $LATEST suffix or the version number as suffix to the function ARN.Lambda only publishes a new function version if the code has never been published or if the code has changed compared to the most recently published version

Reference: https://docs.aws.amazon.com/lambda/latest/dg/configuration-versions.html

Answer 163: D

CloudWatch Logs allows one to store log data indefinitely. CloudWatch metrics can be set up for storage for up to 15 months. CloudWatch does not support metric deletion. Metrics expire based on the retention schedules described above.

Reference: https://aws.amazon.com/cloudwatch/faqs/

Answer 164: A

Alexa service only supports OAuth 2.0 authorization protocol for account linking.

Reference: https://developer.amazon.com/docs/account-linking/how-account-linking-works.html

Answer 165: A

Wake word can be selected from one of the pre-defined works (Alexa, Echo, Amazon, Computer) from the Alexa app settings. Users can enable or disable a skill in the Alexa app, as well as link or unlink accounts.

https://www.amazon.com/gp/help/customer/display.html?nodeId=201549940

Answer 166: A

The Smart Home Skill API can define requests for a skill using device directives for a smart home camera feed. Being a pre-built model with supported device directive for the action (camera feed), its much simpler than creating a custom skill.

https://developer.amazon.com/en-US/docs/alexa/ask-overviews/build-skills-with-the-alexa-skills-kit.html#what-kind-of-skill-do-you-want-to-create

Answer 167: D

If a built-in slot type is fit for purpose but missing some values required or need to add additional values, the easiest thing to do is to add your own custom values to the built-in list slot types. This appends the values you provide to the built-in values defined by Amazon, and yet retains all the validations associated with the slot type. Most built-int slot types can be extended, including AMAZON.Movie.

Reference: https://developer.amazon.com/en-US/docs/alexa/custom-skills/slot-type-reference.html#list-types

Answer 168: C

The standard Response objects methods are outputSpeech, card, reprompt, shouldEndSession, in addition to device specific directives.

Reference: https://developer.amazon.com/docs/custom-skills/request-and-response-json-reference.html#response-object

Answer 169: C

Any skill using the Alexa Location Services must include a link to the skill's Privacy Policy on the Distribution page of the developer console.
The skill must not be a child-directed skill.
The skill must obtain the latest location information every time the customer invokes the skill with a request that needs this information, and the skill must overwrite the prior location data it had from the customer's previous request (that is, store only the most recent data). The skill also shouldn't use location information, or other customer information, to link the customer's account in the background.

Reference: https://developer.amazon.com/en-US/docs/alexa/custom-skills/location-services-for-alexa-skills.html#conditions-for-location-services

Answer 170: B

The Gadget Controller interface enables skills to control Echo Buttons(e.g. change the color), while the Game Engine interface filters Echo Button presses into named events that it forwards to your skill.

Reference: https://developer.amazon.com/docs/echo-button-skills/understand-echo-button-skills.html#incorporate

Answer 171: D

If the word for a slot value has apostrophes indicating the possessive, or any other similar punctuation (such as periods or hyphens) include those within the brackets defining the slot. So ""{slot}'s"", ""{slot}-something"" or ""{slot}.something"", etc. all are invalid slot declarations.
Refer to all limitations below:

https://developer.amazon.com/docs/custom-skills/create-intents-utterances-and-slots.html#h3_intentref_rules

Answer 172: C

Designating a required slot as requiring confirmation is optional.

Slot validation rules can be created for both required and non-required slots.

The Skill Builder can specify that the entire intent requires confirmation, this will enable confirmation for all slots filled in by the user.

The skill builder can control the order in which Alexa asks for each required slot value (in the Intent Slots section of the intent detail page).

https://developer.amazon.com/docs/custom-skills/define-the-dialog-to-collect-and-confirm-required-information.html#dialog-model-components

Answer 173: A

Users invoke a custom skill by using a phrase (supported by the Alexa service) in combination with the invocation name, and request for information ("Alexa, ask Daily Horoscopes for the horoscope for Gemini").

Here it follows the pattern: *<phrase><intent> <slot value>< <invocation name>*

Reference: https://developer.amazon.com/docs/custom-skills/understanding-how-users-invoke-custom-skills.html

Answer 174: D

Refer below to the list of SSML tags supported by Alexa Skills Kit.

https://developer.amazon.com/en-US/docs/alexa/custom-skills/speech-synthesis-markup-language-ssml-reference.html#ssml-supported

Answer 175: B

An IntentRequest can include multiple possible matches for a slot rather than just one (The values array within resolutionsPerAuthority contains the possible matching slot values).

When using a built-in slot type "as-is", no entity resolution takes place, but Entity Resolution takes place if a built-in slot type is extended with additional values.

To test a skill with entity resolution without a device, a skill builder can use the Test page in the developer console.

Reference: https://developer.amazon.com/docs/custom-skills/define-synonyms-and-ids-for-slot-type-values-entity-resolution.html

Answer 176: A

You can extend the standard built-in intents by providing additional sample utterances. You can also implement the built-in intent but extending the built-in one to include the required utterances is the easiest thing to do.

Reference: https://developer.amazon.com/docs/custom-skills/implement-the-built-in-intents.html#extending

Answer 177: D

The in-skill product types are: Consumables, subscriptions and One-time Purchases

https://developer.amazon.com/docs/in-skill-purchase/isp-overview.html#create-isp

Answer 178: B, D

The interfaces required for a basic music interface are Alexa.Media.Search GetPlayableContent, Alexa.Media.Playback Initiate, Alexa.Media.PlayQueue GetItem.

Reference: https://developer.amazon.com/docs/music-skills/api-reference-overview.html#interfaces-for-a-voice-control-experience

Answer 179: B, D

A beta test can accommodate upto 500 users, can last upto 90 days, and can be used to collect feedback from users. A skill may or may not be certified to be eligible for beta-testing, however, only one version (live or beta) can be available to users at any point of time.

https://developer.amazon.com/docs/custom-skills/skills-beta-testing-for-alexa-skills.html#faq-for-the-skill-beta-testing-tool

Answer 180: C

Each lambda alias has a unique ARN, which can only point to a function version, not another alias. An alias can point to a maximum of two Lambda function versions, provided both versions have the same IAM execution role, both have the same dead-

letter queue configuration (if set up) and both versions are published. The alias can only point to a specific function version and cannot point to $LATEST. One can update an alias to point to a new version of the function.

Reference: https://docs.aws.amazon.com/lambda/latest/dg/configuration-aliases.html#using-aliases

Answer 181: A

CloudFront is a Content Distribution Network which speeds up distribution of static and dynamic web content to users, by routing the user to the nearest data center (edge location), providing the lowest latency and best possible performance

https://docs.aws.amazon.com/AmazonCloudFront/latest/DeveloperGuide/Introduction.html

Answer 182: D

The Alexa supported SSML tags are :
"amazon:effect,audio,break,emphasis,lang,p,phoneme,prosody,s,say-as,speak,sub,voice,w"

https://developer.amazon.com/docs/custom-skills/speech-synthesis-markup-language-ssml-reference.html#ssml-supported

Answer 183: A

Policy violations, if any, will be found during testing. Configuration changes to a live skill is not possible. To change any configuration or interaction model of the live skill, the development version of the live skill needs to be updated and sent for certification.

Reference: https://developer.amazon.com/docs/devconsole/test-and-submit-your-skill.html#revise-and-update

Answer 184: B

Amazon CloudWatch provides logging and metric alerting, none of the other AWS resources mentioned provide any alerting capabilities, though S3 and DynamoDB provide some logging capabilities.

https://developer.amazon.com/es/blogs/alexa/post/99fb071e-9aaf-481b-b9af-0186c0f712a5/how-to-monitor-custom-alexa-skills-using-amazon-cloudwatch-alarms

Answer 185: B

"Voice" tag gives the option to (select and) speak with one of the available Amazon Polly voices. All other options are significantly more time and effort consuming. Speak is the root element of an SSML document and does not have any attributes.

https://developer.amazon.com/docs/custom-skills/speech-synthesis-markup-language-ssml-reference.html#voice

Answer 186: B

Refer to the four types of roles you can set for users (Administrator, Marketer, Analyst, Developer) and their permissions below:

https://developer.amazon.com/docs/app-submission/manage-account-and-permissions.html#add_other_users

Answer 187: C

A Smart Home Skill does not need invocation name, they are enabled by searching for the skill name on the Alexa App and account linking to the device cloud.

Reference: https://developer.amazon.com/en-US/docs/alexa/smarthome/steps-to-build-a-smart-home-skill.html

Answer 188: B

A list skill can only be created using the ASK CLI .

https://developer.amazon.com/docs/smapi/steps-to-create-a-list-skill.html

Answer 189: D

Skills may include audio messaging informing customers of promotional offers or deals in response to specific requests from customers. A skill cannot explicitly request a user to leave a positive rating for the skill but can request to leave a review or rating. A skill that allows customers to search web content must search with a specific online resource and attribute the source of information, and the provided answers must not

violate Alexa content policies. Child-directed skill can't sell any physical products or services but can sell digital products or services using ISP.

Reference: https://developer.amazon.com/en-US/docs/alexa/custom-skills/policy-testing-for-an-alexa-skill.html

Answer 190: D

Actions metrics is only available for Smart Home skills

https://developer.amazon.com/en-US/docs/alexa/devconsole/measure-skill-usage.html#skill-metrics

Answer 191: C, D

The following skills are not activated by an invocation name: Smart Home Skill, Video Skill , Flash Briefing Skill. Custom skills use an invocation name (exception being enabling Alexa to search for a skill to fulfill a customer's request using CanFulfillIntentRequest)

Reference: https://developer.amazon.com/en-US/docs/alexa/ask-overviews/understanding-how-users-interact-with-skills.html#examples-of-interaction-models

Answer 192: B

In-Skill Purchase Interface, via the addDirective() method, supports the following actions: Buy, Cancel, Upsell

Reference: https://developer.amazon.com/docs/alexa-skills-kit-sdk-for-nodejs/call-alexa-service-apis.html#in-skill-purchase-interface

Answer 193: A, B

The Alexa App shows the skill card and the skill usage history

Reference: https://developer.amazon.com/en-US/docs/alexa/custom-skills/test-and-debug-a-custom-skill.html#h2_testapp

Answer 194: A

For a skill to work, it must be distributed in the region to be used and support the language to be used in the user device. You should deploy your code to multiple endpoints (based on location) for latency reasons, but this is not a must.

https://developer.amazon.com/en-US/docs/alexa/devconsole/launch-your-skill.html#select-countries-and-regions-for-the-skill

Answer 195: D

This object can only be included when sending a response to a CanFulfillIntentRequest, LaunchRequest, IntentRequest, Display.ElementSelected request or an InputHandlerEvent.
Reference: https://developer.amazon.com/en-US/docs/alexa/custom-skills/request-and-response-json-reference.html#outputspeech-object

Answer 196: C

The PlaybackController interface provides requests to notify your skill when the user interacts with player controls, such as the buttons on a device, a remote control, or the next/previous touch controls on an Alexa-enabled device with a screen. Your skill can respond to these requests with AudioPlayer directives to start and stop playback.
https://developer.amazon.com/docs/custom-skills/playback-controller-interface-reference.html

Answer 197: B

Phoneme provides a phonemic/phonetic pronunciation for the contained text. When using this tag, Alexa uses the pronunciation provided in the "ph" attribute rather than the text contained within the tag. This allows a way to pronounce words differently.
https://developer.amazon.com/docs/custom-skills/speech-synthesis-markup-language-ssml-reference.html#phoneme

Answer 198: D

You can use the utterance profiler once you have defined and built an interaction model. The utterance profiler does not call an endpoint, so you do not need to develop the service for your skill to test your model. utterance profiler does not support testing slot validation, but supports slot elicitation, slot confirmation, and intent confirmation.

https://developer.amazon.com/en-US/docs/alexa/custom-skills/test-utterances-and-improve-your-interaction-model.html#prerequisites

Answer 199: C

Example phrases must be 100% supported by the sample utterances. The phrase in answer C is fully supported by the sample utterance: "what is the status of my order {orderno}"".

Reference: https://developer.amazon.com/en-US/docs/alexa/custom-skills/create-intents-utterances-and-slots.html#identify-slots

Answer 200: D

When you type test utterances, do not use date abbreviations such as "4/15/2019" Instead, write out the date as it would be spoken.

Reference: https://developer.amazon.com/docs/devconsole/test-your-skill.html#alexa-simulator-limitations

Answer 201: A

Customers can only make in-skill purchases via voice at this time.

For adding ISP support to a skill, you will need to have at least one product for the user to choose, handle the buy or cancel intent, as well as refund request as well. The ISP product types are of type Entitlements, Consumables or Subscriptions.

If a skill offers consumable products, the userId remains the same even if the user disables and re-enables the skill.

Reference: https://developer.amazon.com/docs/in-skill-purchase/add-isps-to-a-skill.html

Answer 202: B

"What's new?" provides a description of the changes in this updated version of your skill. If you leave this field blank, your skill is not shown in the Recently Updated section.

Reference: https://developer.amazon.com/docs/devconsole/launch-your-skill.html#skill-metadata

Answer 203: C

Skill metrics are available using the Metrics API or the Developer Console.

Metrics are not available for meeting skills.

All metrics data excludes invocations from the Test page in the developer console.

Most metrics are available for skills in both the development and live stages for a skill.

For each metric, you can view infographics like charts, grids, or other visualizations that can be exported as PNG or JPEG images or download the raw data in CSV format.

References: https://developer.amazon.com/docs/devconsole/measure-skill-usage.html#faq

https://developer.amazon.com/docs/smapi/metrics-api.html

Answer 204: D

The order in which the skill receives list and skill events sent to skill is not necessarily the same as when they occurred.

Alexa will attempt to redeliver events if an acknowledgement is not sent by the skill service, for up to one hour.

Once a customer links the account with the skill, the access token is included in all subsequent events.

Once a customer grants permission to the skill, the permissions object is added to the user object in all subsequent events. Using the item_id or Alexa_list_id from the event generated, the Skill Developer can identify if an event was generated by their list (or items in the list).

Reference: https://developer.amazon.com/docs/custom-skills/list-faq.html

Answer 205: A

Only custom skill type can be hosted on an external web service, use lambda function for creating a skill based on one of the pre-built skill models.

Reference: https://developer.amazon.com/docs/custom-skills/host-a-custom-skill-as-a-web-service.html

Answer 206: C

Intents, Sample utterances and Slot Types are required to build the Interaction model for a custom skill.

Dialog model is optional and required only to create a multi-turn conversation between your skill and the user to collect all the information needed to fulfill an intent.

Reference: https://developer.amazon.com/docs/custom-skills/create-the-interaction-model-for-your-skill.html

Answer 207: D

Any of the following can be used to manage skill interaction model (including intents and utterances): ASK CLI, SMAPI, Developer Console. AWS Console is for managing AWS infrastructure and resources (including any lambda function associated with a skill).

Reference: https://developer.amazon.com/docs/custom-skills/create-the-interaction-model-for-your-skill.html#build-and-save

Answer 208: A

Because Amazon S3 provides eventual consistency for updates to existing objects, but DynamoDbPersistenceAdapter is recommended for persistent attributes if your skill requires read-after-write consistency. Request attributes only last within a single request processing lifecycle, while Session attributes persist throughout the lifespan of the current skill session

Reference: https://developer.amazon.com/docs/alexa-skills-kit-sdk-for-nodejs/manage-attributes.html